HOW TO CONTROL THAT WHICH CANNOT BE CONTROLLED

A Guide to Network Leadership

Publisher: Karlex Oy
Page layout and graphics: Eve Sillanpää
Translation: Henrik Andergård

ISBN 978-952-65337-6-6 (soft-cover)
ISBN 978-952-65337-7-3 (EPUB)
ISBN 978-952-65337-8-0 (MP3)

KARL-JOHAN SPIIK

COMMUNITY-LED ORIENTATION

How to Control That Which Cannot Be Controlled

A Guide to Network Leadership

KARLEX

CONTENTS

1. FOREWORD

Ice swimmers, families with young children, CEOs, newspaper editors, dog enthusiasts, coders. Humans form networks among themselves, both unofficial and official ones. We talk of social i.e. community-oriented networks: in them, people receive help, ideas, peer support, springboards upwards, and tips regarding new and interesting networks.

During my life I have been part of several different community-oriented networks. The networks have taken shape as I have needed them. When I have wanted something that I have felt I could not attain on my own, I have started creating a network with which I have been able to advance the matter. Networks for various different interests, professional goals, hobbies, and entrepreneurships have appeared in my life.

All these human networks work the same way, because the contributing factor are humans themselves.

In primary school I formed friendship networks so that I could express myself and make friends, even though I didn't yet know anything about networking. In upper secondary school I created study and hobby networks, so that I could find a counterweight to my studies. During my military service I formed support networks, so that I could be able to live happily within the army's leadership system. During my studies I created a peer network by taking photographs and bringing people together in the nightlife.

My career was headed towards the IT field, where people worked in networked and community-oriented ways. As my career progressed, I started to understand how important it is to give people responsibility and power, because then people become motivated by what they are doing. Having acted in networks for over three decades, I wanted to write a book about how networks are led and what they consist of.

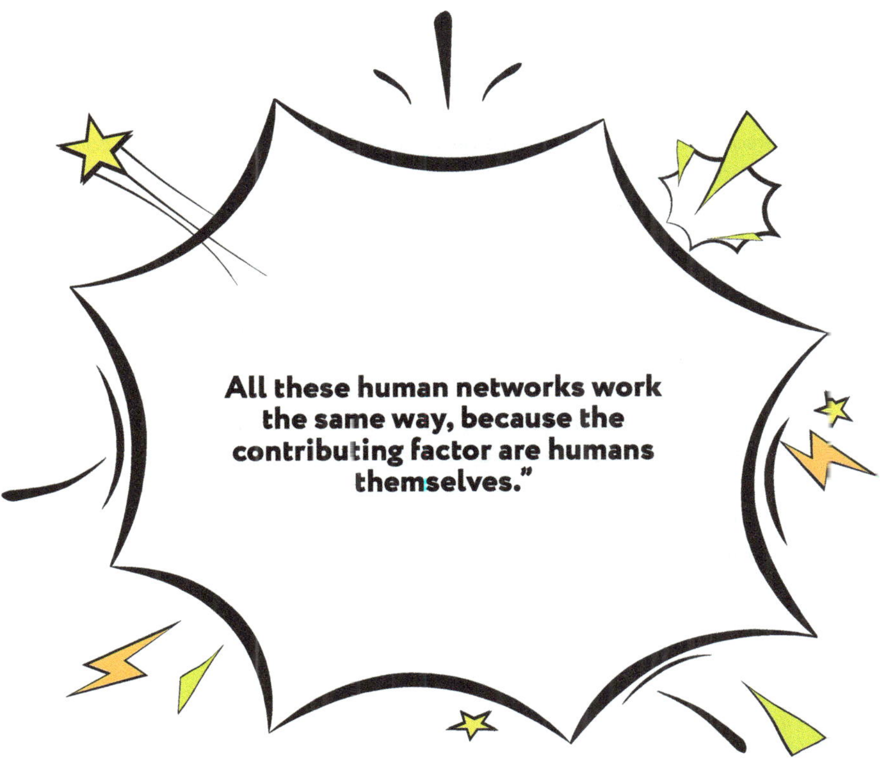

All these human networks work the same way, because the contributing factor are humans themselves."

2. INTRODUCTION

Leading a network means that you influence what people do despite not having the title of leader nor even necessarily being the most experienced person in the group. Leading a network requires taking others into consideration, doing favours, acting as adjudicator, honesty, and an attitude that others can identify with and trust.

Leading a network exposes the person to critique, because leadership cannot be performed from the shadows. The position of network leader can also easily be lost if one tries to lead the network by manipulation and a sanctimonious attitude.

In this book I present how to build and maintain various networks. It is essential to recognise people's differences and differing desires to please others. Networks can consist of similar people, but the most efficient networks are those that are diverse, consisting of people different from each other and people from various different backgrounds. In a network you utilise the skills of all the members towards a shared goal.

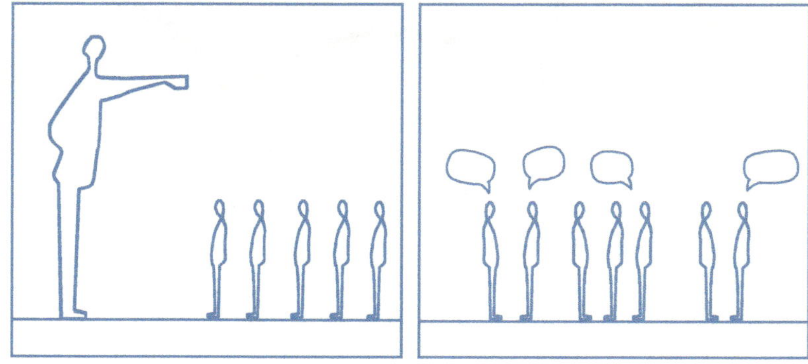

In traditional leadership one person directs others, whereas in network leadership everyone is on the same level.

Networks should feature openness, so that the network doesn't start resembling traditional leadership and giving orders. Information needs to be available to everyone in the network. If it isn't, the leader of the network should create such conventions, with which information can easily be found when needed, and thus the information won't be hidden away with just a small group of people. When activities are open and safe, everyone has a chance to improve themselves. Development of a network happens via fore-runners and guiding others i.e. orientating people.

If information doesn't flow in the network, the activities of the network slow down and soon cease entirely. A network is based on communication.

One should be able to measure and assess the activities of a network, so that it can be developed. In a network, functions cannot be centralised, but rather everyone should be given the opportunity to influence everything. When everyone has access to the network's information and is connected to the other members, everyone can develop the network's activities in the desired direction.

The desired direction is usually determined by what purpose the network serves. It can for instance serve its members or an outside group. Thus the network's decisions are always made based on what the network sees as the most important for its activities.

Networks are agile and mutable. Networks cannot feature rigid structures, because otherwise the members might feel that the aims of the network don't suit them any longer. Of course, the members can change, or the network might serve its members only for a specified amount of time, if the activities of the network aren't meant to change. If the activities within the network change as its members change, the network can live almost forever.

Networks do not serve their purpose if their activities always require the presence and approval of certain people. Within networks one has to understand that technology changes the world and people's lives, and thus networks have to keep pace with the change. A network can also not drown people in an information overload or take up all of people's time. Everyone in a network should use their time wisely and communicate it to others. Because of this, it is important to have mutually agreed ways of communicating and of writing things down in a network.

The core of any network is people. Conflicts inevitably occur between people. The most important thing for a network is to learn to recover from conflicts instead of trying to avoid disagreements. People need to be able to bring up problems and discuss them openly.

Manipulation, roles, and silent leadership also all occur within large corporations. These are recognisable phenomena, and there is no need to fear them.

Large organisations often contain several networks within them. Even though the organisation might nominally feature another type of hierarchy and team division, in reality work is always done via networks. Each of us belongs to one or more networks – though some of them might be secret.

The potential of networks is their power and how that power is used.

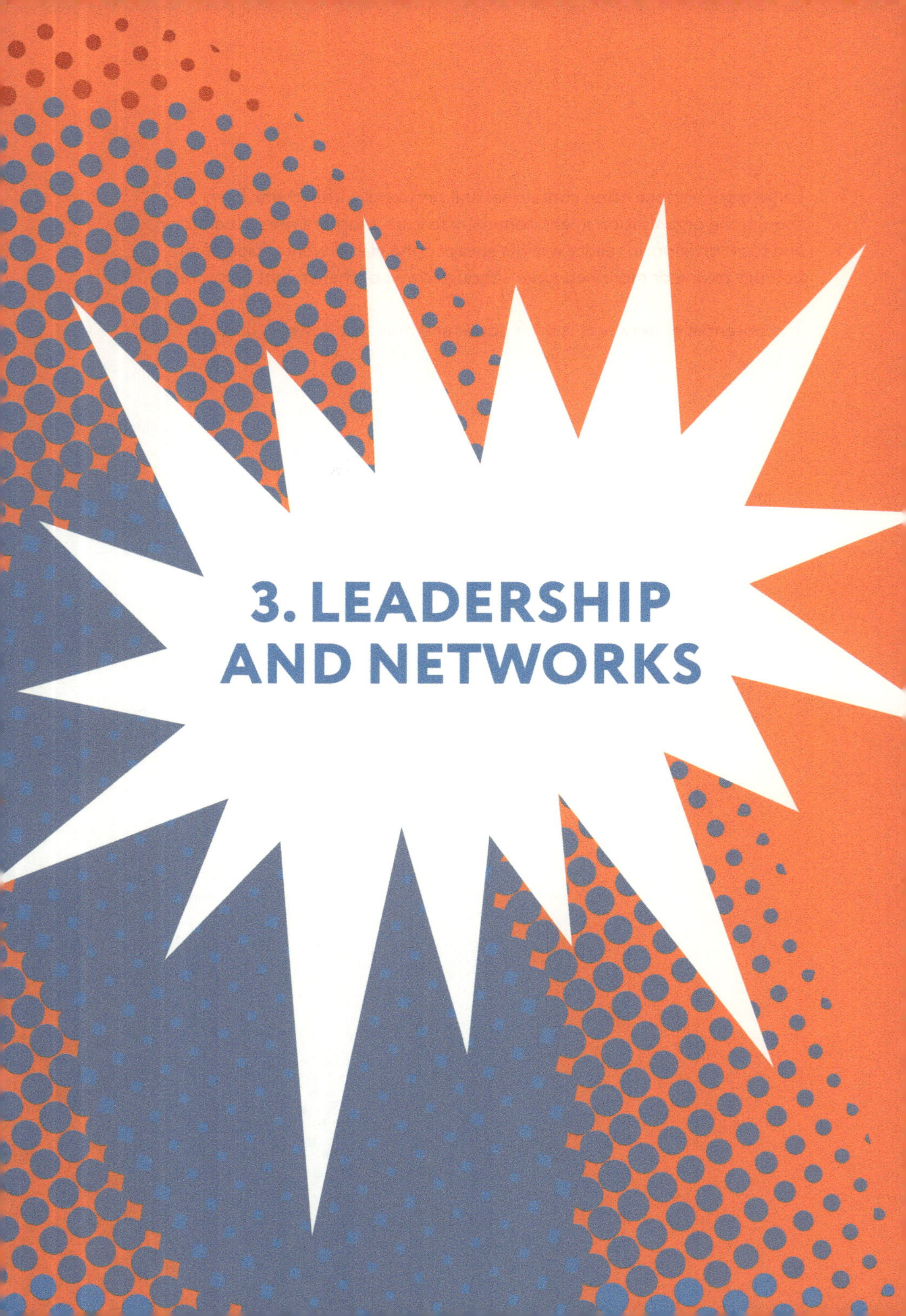

3. LEADERSHIP AND NETWORKS

3.1 What is Community-Led Orientation and How Does It Relate to Networks

In work communities, tasks are always done in networks, even though roles and titles might be defined differently. When the sleeves are rolled up, you work with the people whom you have worked with before and with whom it feels pleasant to work with. People communicate among themselves directly and ask each other things, irrespective of titles or what status anyone has.

With experience, people expand networks in organisations. For example, as a child everyone had their own friend group in the schoolyard. When you played games, you invited others to join in. If someone had older siblings, neighbours, or other acquaintances from outside their own group, there was usually some connection via which you got to know new people, and thus you expanded your own sphere.

This kind of networking is natural, and it happens in work life too. In the break room everyone is equal. A person who is lower in the organisation's hierarchy might unofficially be very well-liked, and might thus become a quiet leader or an opinion leader.

The idea behind community-led orientation is to change the structures and processes of organisations to be more like natural networking.

In a community-oriented organisation superiors and bosses don't make the decisions, but instead they are made by everyone together. In a fully community-oriented organisation there is no hierarchy nor are there any particular titles: people who are interested in various things come together and decide how they want to manage said things. This does not mean chaos, nor that anyone could decide on just about anything, but rather it implies a higher level of flexibility than before.

As an organisation contains more and more people, the need for e.g. personnel management (HR) increases. People are usually selected for HR work based on their interest in the topic. In a traditional organisation, an HR person would be specifically hired to handle personnel management. In a community-oriented organisation, these decisions are instead handled by a group of people who meet up regularly.

Similar groups can be formed for e.g. sales, marketing, and communications. For projects, traditional roles such as project manager, publicist, and workers can be agreed on – or you might agree that the roles are rotated among people. Irrespective of whether it is a process or a project, things are agreed on together and written down. Thus you create a cultural handbook, a set of guidelines, or a process description of how things are done in your organisation. When you wish to change something, it is decided on together, and the documentation is then also updated.

As a new person joins the organisation, they can familiarise themselves with the organisation's cultural handbook: this is how we operate in this organisation.

3.2 What is Shared Leadership and How Does It Differ from Traditional Leadership

Shared leadership means that instead of one person making decisions, several people make the decisions together.

A group of people can also decide that one person can represent them and make decisions on their behalf. This way various roles can be created in the group. For instance, in project-type work it is good to give different responsibilities to different people, so that everyone isn't needlessly working on the same things.

Matters relating to the group's or organisation's core operations are usually decided on together, whereas e.g. communications can be entrusted to the person whose written and spoken communicative skills are the best. Everyone can apply for a role or a group which best reflects their strengths. It is good that everyone in a community has the chance to join groups based on their interests, for instance if someone wants to practice sales or HR tasks.

When you have figured out who are part of the organisation's core operations and who are part of the various functions supporting these core operations – such as HR, sales, marketing or communications – you need to create the framework for decision-making. Are decisions made via voting, in small groups, or is power given to the individuals, who just notify the others about the decisions they've made? Limits can of course be set on decision-making: for instance, everyone might be allowed to independently decide on purchases smaller than 100 €, but larger expenses should be confirmed with one's team or project group.

One of the benefits of shared leadership is that these decisions are made among those who are doing the actual work.

There are often several different methods of decision-making within an organisation. It's good to write down these methods, so that you can always refer back to the notes if necessary, to check what was agreed on. If some method is found to be bad, a new approach can be tried out at the drop of a hat, as long as a majority of people agrees with it.

When decisions are made together, no one can cause disruptions or bully others. If you want to carry out your own desire, you have to discuss it with the others and get them to understand your point of view. Often one's own point of view might even change during the process.

When things are discussed in a group, the ideas of every participant get included. This also commits people to decisions, because everyone feels that they got a chance to influence the decisions.

Everyone does not have to make decisions. It is okay to abstain yourself and say that you're not interested in making a decision on a given matter. However, you then have to remember that it is no use complaining if you don't like the decision that others make on the matter. Everyone should have the chance to influence decisions that affect their own work – this is shared leadership.

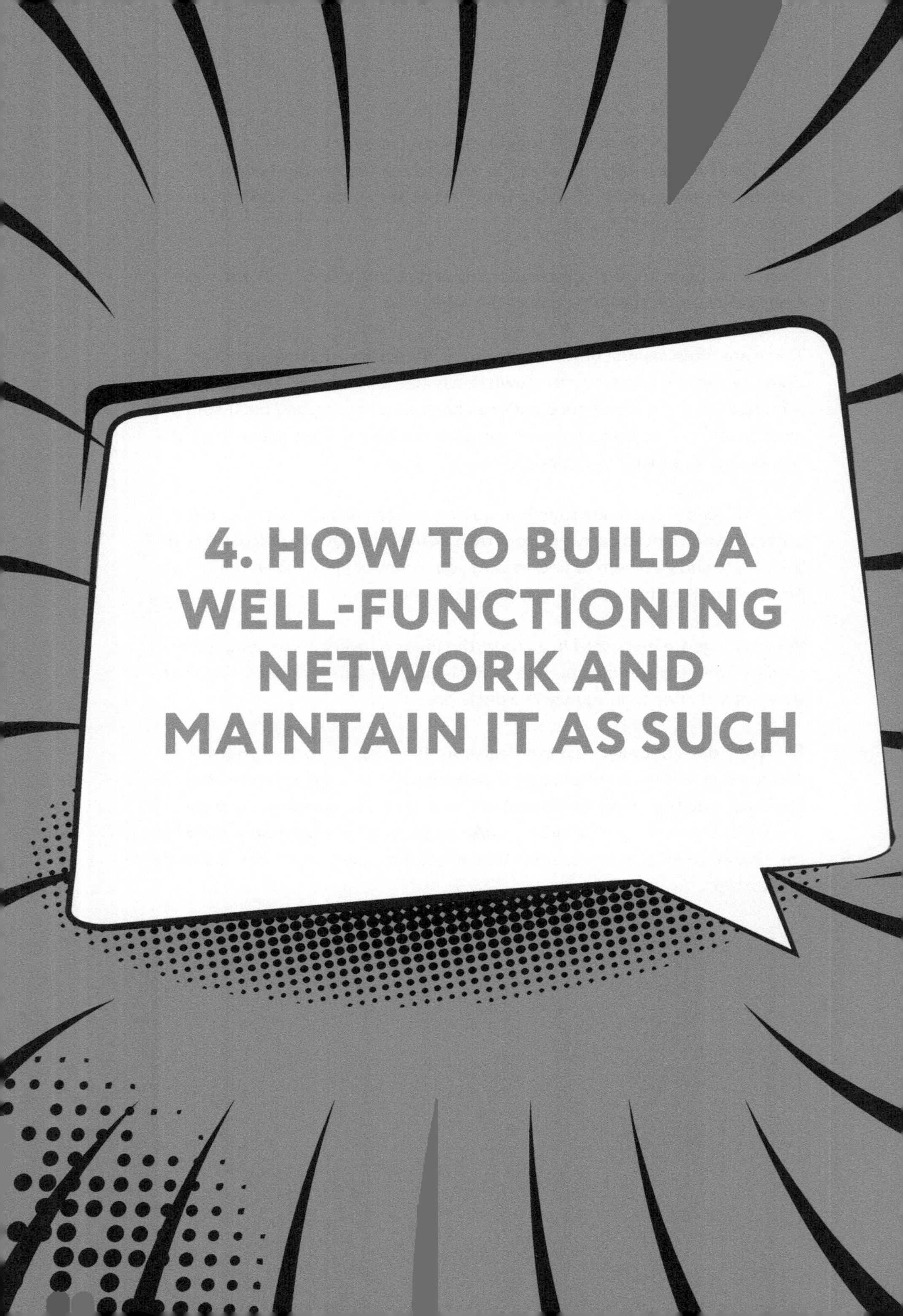

4. HOW TO BUILD A WELL-FUNCTIONING NETWORK AND MAINTAIN IT AS SUCH

4.1 The Diversity of People

The core of networks are people. If you really aren't interested in other people, you need to charm them by committing to a shared passion, goal or core activity. When you meet people with the same values, you can't help but slowly get interested in others – whether you are a people- or facts-focused person.

It is important to respect others and understand that we are all different. On the other hand, everyone's opinions are not equal, because people's level of competence varies. During discussions you have to manage to make everyone feel important when they are part of the network.

In our previous book Community-Led Orientation – Can You Tolerate People That Are Different than You (note: currently only available in Finnish, titled Yhteisöohjautuvuus – Kestätkö ihmisiä, jotka ovat erilaisia kuin sinä) we presented the four-quadrant theory. In the book, people were grouped based on how people- or facts-focused and how dominant or accommodating they are. The four-quadrant in question and its different personalities is found in the following illustration.

This type of four-quadrant theory is a well-known trait theory, with which it is easy to quickly understand how to work with people who are very different to yourself.

The four-quadrant theory is of course just a theory. It's necessary to make some generalisations in order to get more widely-applicable tools for working with others and for learning to tolerate and appreciate diversity. This division into quarters inevitably has its own flaws, but it's a great tool for when you need to quickly find out how to give feedback or give thanks, how to ask something of a type of person different to yourself, or how to motivate people and get them to cooperate. The style of communication that you prefer might be seen as insulting and even disheartening by one person, whereas another person might find it outright inspiring. A third person might not even realise that you've given them feedback.

People also have differing ways of reacting to stress and differing needs for retaining control. Even being in their work role might cause constant stress, i.e. a state of hypervigilance, to some. The stress might be caused by a poorly-defined and too busy job. Some people are used to retaining control of things for themselves more than others, which may cause them states of hypervigilance when they have to make decisions together with other people.

Stress is necessary, and in short intervals it increases performance, but when it becomes long-lasting, it is only a detriment. Stress changes a person and accentuates the negative aspects of them. For instance, heavy stress might turn a mild and accommodating person more domineering and rude, i.e. place them in a different quadrant of the four-quadrant theory than usual.

A person's behaviour might differ from how they usually behave due to other reasons as well. Their upbringing or the community's social atmosphere might have forced them to hide their social side and act aggressively. It is well-known that when alcohol dampens the inhibitions in the cerebral cortex, quiet and uptight people might suddenly turn out to be open and talkative. This sort of opening-up can be reached without intoxicants, if the community is safe and the person wants to come out of their shell.

When you're assessing a person and pondering how to express things to them, it's worth taking note of the setting. If you can't help them relieve stress in any other way, change the setting and try to make the situation calm and safe. This way you can better meet the other person and go through the relevant matters with them.

4.2 Pleasing Others and Building Relationships

Observing the nature of others and adjusting your own communication to meet them is a form of pleasing. It's important to recognise the people who want direct feedback as well as those who prefer feedback to be given one-on-one. This is not manipulating, but rather it's taking others into consideration. Working in a network often requires pleasing others so that you can focus on the matters at hand and create interpersonal relationships, which are necessary for networks.

Creating interpersonal relationships requires that you properly meet the other person. When working from home, it is generally seen as a good idea to meet up face-to-face during the early stages of a project, job or other mutual activity. You exchange opinions and look for shared values and a common goal. This way you can build an interpersonal relationship with another person. This helps even during difficult times, when communication is sparse and limited, and there's no time to explain things. It's a lot easier to be forgiven for rude behaviour when there's a warm relationship as a foundation.

Your own status will never mean that you don't have to please others or take their personalities or situations into consideration. If the organisation or situation has roles in which it is possible to dictate procedures, tasks, and requests, it is sadly all too easy to then forget to take others into consideration. In networks where you are at least nominally equal to each other, interpersonal relations and open communication becomes highly important.

You cannot lead a network by commanding. You have to agree on things together and involve people.

4.3 The Network Has to Be Open to Diversity

The members of the group differ from each other in terms of e.g. gender, age, health, sexual orientation, social class, disabilities, religion, nationality, linguistic background, or values. Leading a network requires taking this diversity into consideration as well as pondering whether it should be increased or e.g. talked about.

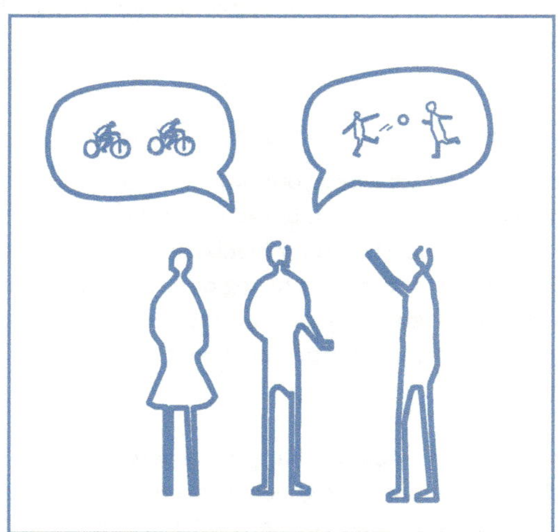

Networks naturally form around shared interests. In network leadership, you have to be able to include various kinds of people, so that the network becomes diverse.

In hobby networks, the uniting factor is the hobby. For instance, in a boating network people share a common interest in boating. At the same time, the network excludes e.g. people with mobility impairments, with too small an income, or whose childhood never included boat travel. The same is true at the workplace. It is not in itself a bad thing that similar people with similar attitudes cluster together around a shared interest. However, it does limit the group's ability to think about things from a wider perspective or to accept differing opinions and points of view. It is good for the network leader to be able to bring these things up if the network's homogeneity starts to become a detriment to the group's functioning.

Other networks are naturally diverse, and thus opinions and the things to be discussed receive several different points of view. It's the network leader's responsibility to encourage and uphold openness, so that no one's background can lead to discrimination or prevent ideas.

A multicultural and diverse network produces the most varied results, but working together can be stormy and might contain various conflicts. It's the network leader's job to help the group recover from conflicts and to emphasize, that we're in fact supposed to be diverse.

Despite the group's diversity, the network leader should manage to create a culture where everyone feels that they are a part of the group and appreciated in the scope of their own role. At the same time the leader should know themselves and accept themselves. If you're not comfortable with yourself, it can be very difficult to accept diversity in others or to find any common ground with narrow-minded people.

4.4 Utilizing Skills

All of us have some skills related to a given network as well as skills that we use outside the network in question. When a person gets to express themselves, they use all of this skill palette of theirs and they apply their skills from various different fields.

Networks need multi-talented people as well as those with precise skills in a specific field. It's good for the network leader to get to know the members of their network and their specialised skills: then the leader can better unite different people to cooperate on things.

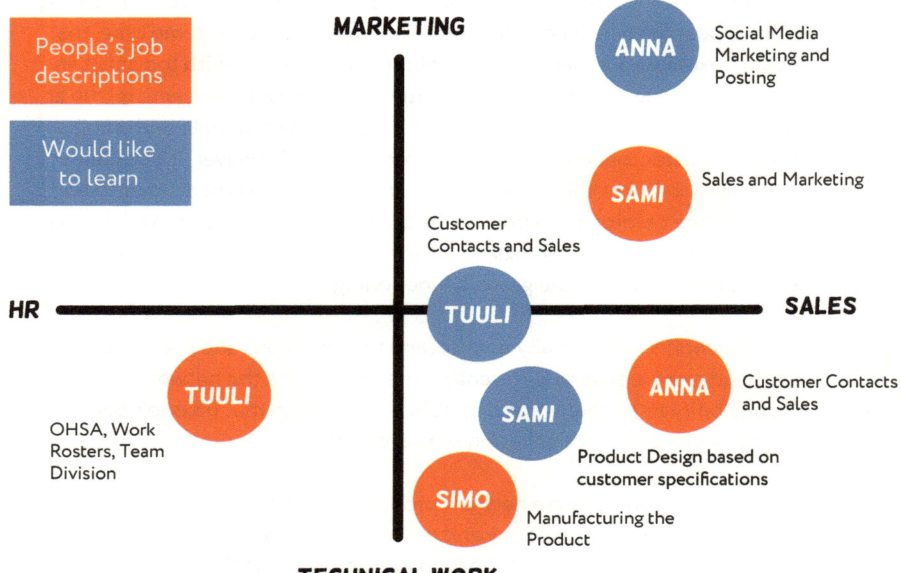

A skills map of the people in a team. What each person is currently doing is shown in red, and what each person would like to learn is shown in blue. A skills map is a tool for new situations in which you have to decide who to ask for help from or who to ask to participate in the task at hand.

You can easily map out a network's skills via IT and communication technology. This, however, does not replace the conversations in which you get to know the others and create a skills map together.

A skills map is a tool with which you show the skills of the network's members. When you encounter a situation where you need a new kind of perspective, you can easily find people's specialised skills on the map. A good skills map is digital, and it has a clear search function. This way each member of the network is able to find and utilise others' skills efficiently.

Utilising the skills of different people requires the ability to motivate people. A detail-oriented person can be motivated by explaining the details to them and giving them a challenge: a detail-oriented person can't resist the temptation to solve the challenge. On the other hand, a big-picture type of skillset requires an entirely different sort of motivating. This is why understanding the diversity among people is an important part of utilising skills and know-how. You can seldom order or demand in a network – and even when you can order or demand, it's still usually better to motivate and please others.

The best way to utilise people's skills is to give everyone a chance to influence the work. This does not mean that you always have to do what everyone wants, but that you ask everyone for their opinion.

Getting opinions, discussion, and clarification require time. Some perspectives naturally fall away as a result of discussing the issue, other perspectives combine, and ultimately a reasonable way of working starts to take shape. The people who participated are motivated, because they see the matter as their own and feel they are doing what's important to them.

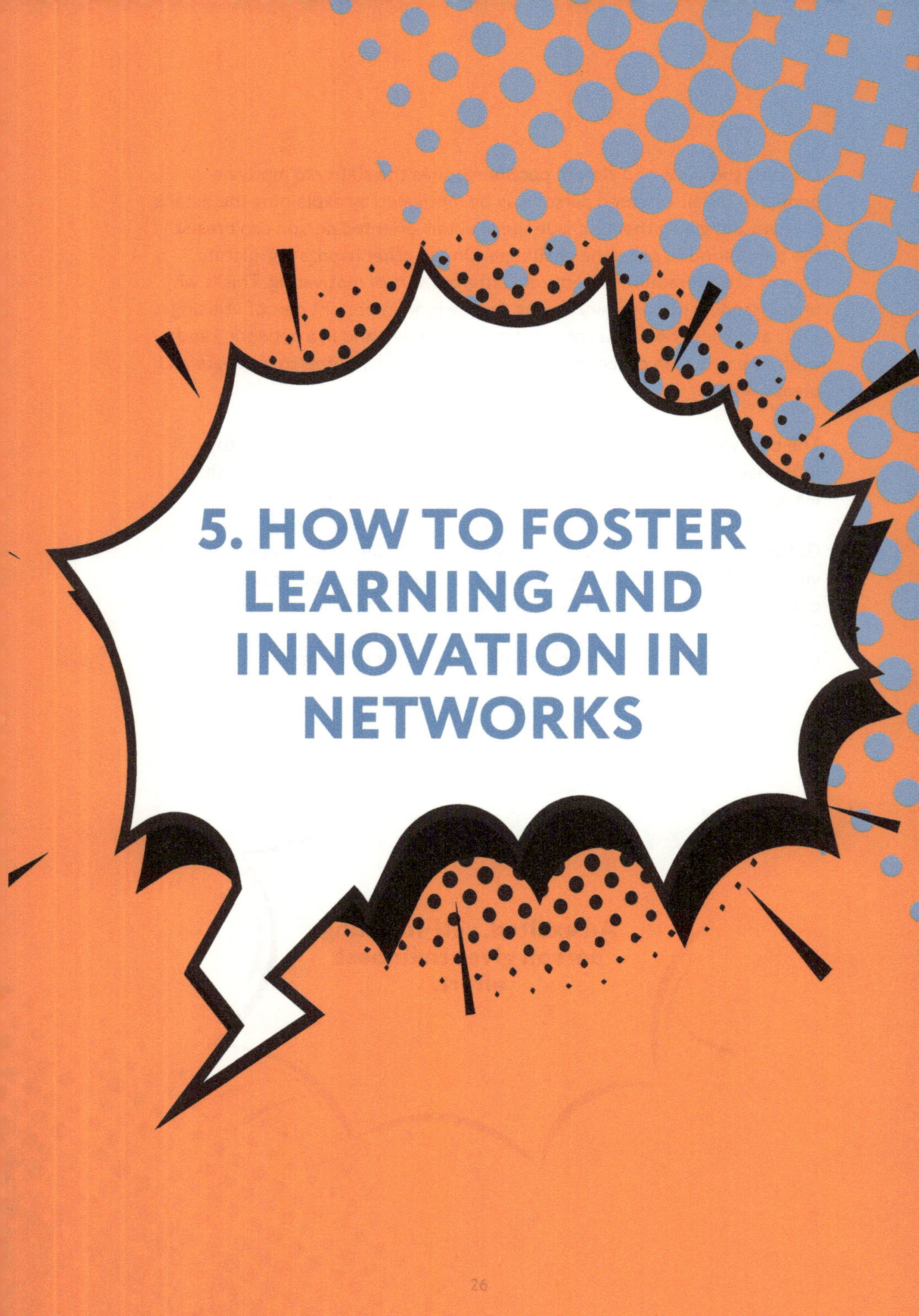
5. HOW TO FOSTER LEARNING AND INNOVATION IN NETWORKS

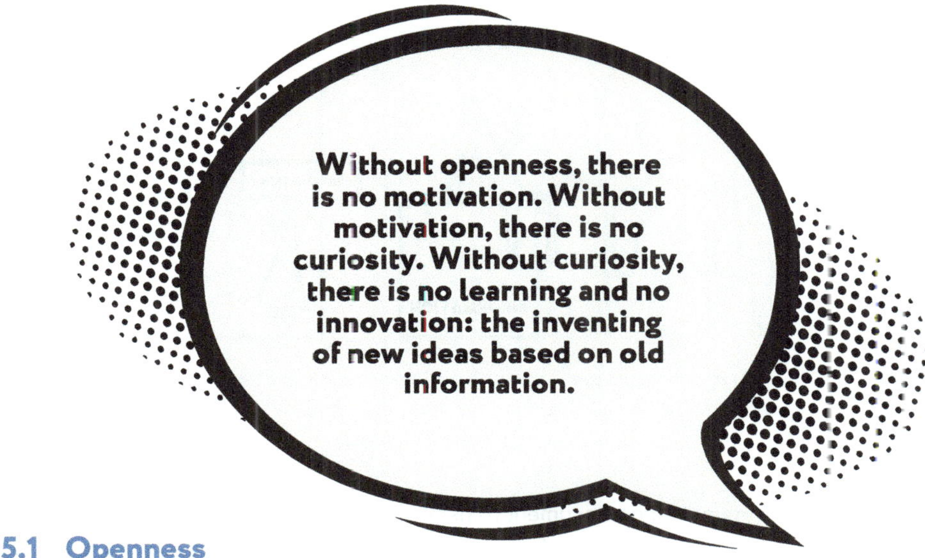

5.1 Openness

Many people have a habit of leaving things unsaid. Some people want to protect others from unnecessary information overload, or might for some other reason withhold informatior. People in a supervisor position or project leadership role might not say, how far along the project is, and things are only reported when all the decisions have already been made. This is harmful to the network leadership, in which all information should be open.

Openness does not mean drowning others in information. Projects, endeavours and other things need to have proper places for information to be stored and where it is shared. This way people can access the information when they want to, but it is not forced on them e.g. via e-mail.

In the book Community-Led Leadership: How Shared Leadership is Created and What Its Requirements Are I discuss agile leadership. Agile leadership is based on task lists, via which information is distributed and tasks are coordinated.

When things are found in their proper places, people have time to find things out and do their jobs. Other people might not be interested in all the organisation's news, developments, and strategic decisions – let's give these people the right to focus on their work and to do it well. E-mail is a tool of the 1990's, and it should not be used for the organisation's internal

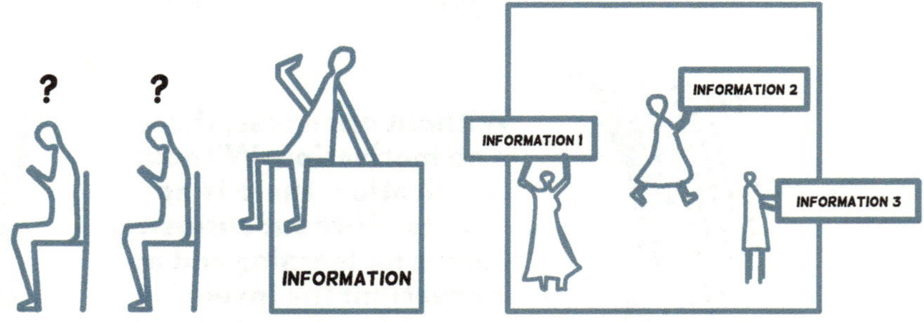

In networks, a leader can't control through information and distribute it as needed. The power of networks is that information is available to everyone, and a person who can combine the information can lead the whole.

communications, document transfer, discussions, nor for any other purposes. Nowadays there are better tools available for these tasks. These tools are presented more in-depth in the book Community-Led Team: How to Create a Team That Leads Itself.

A team leader does not have to know everything. Far too often, the project leader might during a meeting admit that they've not had time to deal with various tasks relating to the project. In these situations it's worth considering whether the correct person is in charge of dealing with those tasks or not. In the name of openness, there could be a discussion about whether someone else would be able to take on the responsibility for these tasks that have until now been the leader's responsibility. If a clear task list is being used, the details and descriptions of the project are already written down, and delegating the tasks to someone else is easy.

One thing that might be an obstacle for openness is that people haven't learned to write things down. People are used to keeping information in their own head and dealing with things when it suits them. This is burdensome: information is splintered between memory, e-mail, and various corridor talks. This sort of working is not open, but closed. Openness necessitates documentation and managing your own work, so that the network always has the necessary information about current affairs.

People's readiness to note things down will of course vary: someone might note things down so concisely, that others can't understand the notes; another person writes so long novels, that others don't have time to familiarise themselves with the notes. At first the quality might vary, but with time the results even out, and "our way" of noting things down develops. It cannot develop if it is never practiced or never begun.

When all the information in an organisation or network is open, the members can draw conclusions and make decisions based on it. By opening up the company's financial figures to the personnel and by creating clear indicators for measuring e.g. the order backlog, the profit, and the performance in different fields, you can show those interested how the company's finances are doing. Every interested individual can find out the things they want to know and learn from them.

A belief that has gotten entrenched in many organisations is that it's not a good idea to open up unfinished and complex topics to employees out of fear of misuse, undue indignation, or disappointment. False perceptions can of course spread far. On the other hand, openness is the only way to develop a network, even if there might initially be problems. By thinking on behalf of others, by sheltering and patronizing others you cannot get forward.

5.2 Information Location and Data Security

If all information in a network is encrypted, hidden, or if you always have to request it from others, people's motivation will quickly wane. There are different types of people in a network: some people might immediately want to start working on things when they become inspired. If they at this point have to ask for authorisation and wait for hours, days, or weeks, the enthusiasm will be gone by the time access is granted. Furthermore, work will become disorganised and slow, as things cannot be finished in one go. Because of this, you have to carefully choose where to store the information which the network needs and who is given access to it.

The information used in a network should by default be accessible to everyone, and access should only be limited to explicitly confidential information – not the other way around. The network's or organisation's data storage solution needs to be chosen with this in mind.

Data security does of course need to be managed, so that no one inadvertently shares the network's information to the wrong entities. The network must together decide what information is permitted to be shared and what isn't, and these decisions must be documented.

Europe has adopted the GDPR, and elsewhere in the world various equivalent regulations exist regarding data storage. In practice, the purpose of these regulations is to ensure that if you are storing social security numbers or bank account numbers, your data security needs to be well-designed. If you are storing any personal information in general, you have to make sure that the information isn't leaked. This is usually handled well enough within organisations, but in networks the activities might extend across organisational boundaries.

People use instant messaging software and e-mail for personal communication, and the data security of these formats is not particularly good. In a worst-case scenario, a network might revolve around one WhatsApp group, which means information storage and management is chaotic and data security is in shambles. It's difficult to find important things in the group, documents cannot be worked on together, and the conversation features both up-to-date and outdated versions of the same information. E-mail features many of the same problems. Better alternatives are e.g. Teams, Slack, or other thread-based communication solutions, which also feature document management solutions.

If you happen to have a brilliant idea during a corridor talk or e.g. in a WhatsApp conversation, you have to have agreed on who should note down the matter in the official database. In a network, you should not idly think that information will spread to others by itself, and you should not accept that the network's databases are constantly a bit deficient and outdated.

In large organisations, people have been trained in communicating securely and in using proper types of databases. In smaller organisations, this might have been forgotten, or the issue might not have been seen as important. In associations, things are usually done during one's free time, and people generally want to save time, so sometimes important information is found e.g. in a comment of a comment in a Facebook group, and at other times in an e-mail or a text message. The fragmentation of information does not aid the association's activities, but instead makes cooperation seem difficult. Interest in continuing the hobby might peter out solely because it's difficult to stay up-to-date on things.

5.3   Pioneers and Orientation

When we talk about networks, particularly about hobby networks, we are
competing for people's free time. Involving people in the activity might become jeopardised if they have to learn new systems such as Teams or Slack,
which were recommended in the previous chapter. On the other hand, there
is the risk of the activities becoming chaotic and difficult if you lack good
ways of managing information.

An advantage of work-based networks is that people spend more time per
day doing work than they do on hobbies. In theory, they have more time to
learn new methods of communicating. On the other hand, people might be
so busy at work that it is difficult to organise time for learning new systems,
or they might not have time to implement the knowledge they gained from
the training sessions.

Irrespective of what methods the network uses to communicate, you always
need pioneers: those who are excited about new things and about getting
to do something among the first or about "putting things in order". The role
of pioneers is noteworthy, because they can achieve a lot very quickly in
networks.

A problem that might emerge in networks is that no progress is made on
anything unless specific people are present. These people form bottlenecks.

A solution to the bottleneck problem is that information is always kept
open, and everyone is able to make decisions, or gather others to make decisions together. When anyone can be a pioneer, the load of the particularly
burdened people gets lighter. All of this can happen by itself, but often these
things need to be specifically raised in order to make people aware of them.
It is important for the pioneers and experienced people to understand that it
is about the network's learning.

The members of a network need to be informed about and instructed in
why things are done the way they are in our network. The network needs
to create some form of orientation, in which the methods of working are
sufficiently explained. However, the orientation needs to emphasize that
these methods can be changed and that the network is open to trying new

In networks, pioneers inspire others and guide them to new activities by the pioneer's own example.

things – as long as data security and work efficiency are maintained in proper proportions.

At its lightest, the orientation might be one file in which the network's modes of operation are noted down, along with the underlying reasons for working in this way. A new person joining the network should confirm that they have read this document.

An orientation might sound like a cumbersome procedure in an agile spare time network, such as a shared vacation trip or a casual football team. However, at some point the network will have to consider its shared habits, and this would be a good time to write them down. This is often done by a pioneer, who acts as an example for others regarding how we function in our network. The exemplary activity of the pioneers also naturally becomes the mode of operation for the networks.

5.4   The Freedom to Learn

If the network exists within an organisation, it is important to give people time to learn more skills and use the network's work time for learning. At the same time, it is reasonable to ask that people might at least to some extent abridge what they've learned for sharing with others in the network.

A network does not learn if the members have to use their free time for learning. A mere interest is often not enough. You have to encourage learning.

Many imagine that learning only means long-winded cramming and reading. A much more common form is micro-learning, which happens all the time without people realising: when we don't know how to do something, we ask for help or look for the relevant information using IT, and we learn. Emphasising this kind of learning is crucial. The network should have some channel for people to store information about what they have learned, since this also brings forth the enthusiasm: "I learned something".

Learning new things should be emphasised and the process of learning needs to be made pleasant. It is good for the network to bring up the idea that we learn together, and that each of us is free to learn more and teach others if we so wish.

Everyone doesn't want to learn new things, and they should also be allowed to work in the way they desire. In networks, you operate by the ideals of mercifulness and encouragement.

The freedom to work in the way you want is the basis of the network's learning. However, responsibility and communication are complements to this freedom. When working in a network, others have to be informed of what you are doing.

It doesn't matter if e.g. there are no shared workspaces nor any shared time. In these situations, you have to build a system that supports other kinds of connections. This could be the club room's notice board or a Teams channel. The specific tool itself doesn't really matter, as long as it has been considered together and it has been taken into use together.

6. WHEN YOU WANT TO MAKE CHANGES TO THE NETWORK'S ACTIVITIES

6.1 Centralising Helps Only on Paper

Centralisation in an organisation means that power and decision-making
gets concentrated to the upper levels, such as upper management or the
head office. Centralisation can be useful when an organisation wants to guarantee a unified strategy or improve quality control. It is easy to believe that
centralisation is efficient, because t can easily be made to look efficient.

Centralisation is a common way to manage things in our society. Companies
have discrete departments that are responsible for e.g. personnel, production, sales, marketing, or finances. Health care is organised into health cent-
res and hospitals, and the elderly are being taken care of in nursing homes.
Schools have only grown and grown. Almost all organisations and operations
have been centralised.

Unfortunately, centralisation is not always efficient. The benefits of centralisation are right in front of our eyes, but the drawbacks often remain hidden.
We don't seem to notice them, because the idea of centralisation is so popu-
lar in our society, and it looks good on paper. We see that when we centralise
operations in a company, we make the processes flow better. We don't see
that centralisation also causes communication problems, lack of trust, and
loss of involvement.

> **I believe that the idea of efficiency through
> centralisation is behind many of the
> problems of the present day. It has become
> like a modern religion whose truth few
> would question. However, centralisation in
> moderation can also be useful, so it should
> not be abandoned completely. The problem
> is when it is continued far beyond the point
> where the drawbacks have already surpassed
> the benefits many times over.**
>
> Topi Jokinen
> oppejaitseohjautuvuudesta.blogspot.com

One of the problems with centralisation is that it takes decision-making
far away from those who feel the repercussions of the decisions. The pain
of bad decisions is not felt by the person who makes the decisions, but by
someone else.

For instance, in a company where sales and production have been separated
into their own departments, it's easy for problems to arise between these
departments. The salespeople might over- or undersell in relation to what
production is capable of. They might also sell something that is difficult for
production to implement. The actions of sales might mess up production,
but the salespeople usually won't have to suffer for this. At worst they might
even get bonuses for the trouble they cause, if production is already overloa-
ded and the salespeople are on commission salaries.

A fundamental problem is that centralising sales and production into their
own departments brings efficiency to both separately. When the salespeople
can focus solely on sales and production can focus solely on production,
both can be optimised for maximum performance. There is, however, a
principle in systemic thinking that explains why this is a problem: if you
optimise the parts, the whole suffers.

In companies, we should above all be interested in the success of the whole.
Why, then, do we so often focus on the parts?

Another problem with centralisation is that it narrows people's opportunities to influence things. You end up creating an organisation that looks
efficient, but which at the same time destroys people's dedication, commu-
nality, and motivation. The problems are easily blamed on the individuals
(people are lazy) instead of realising that the problems are by and large caused by the system. Instead of solving the actual root causes of the problems,
we hire more managers to hold this machinery together.

6.2 Change the Methods of Measuring

In order to be able to assess a network's development, we have to be able to
measure its activities on some level. In order to assess the network's activities, we have to be able to measure what has changed. If we want to develop
the networks' activities, we need to see whether things have changed, and if
so, how quickly.

OLD MEASURING　　　　　　**NEW MEASURING**

A traditional method of measurement forces the respondent into a predetermined setup, while a new method allows the respondent to say what is meaningful.

Usually measuring is done via personnel surveys, i.e. questionnaire forms that ask people certain things, and asks them to grade various things. Measuring has long been very similar. First the things that need to be measured are decided on. Then questions about the topic are created, and a target demographic is chosen. The questionnaires are sent out, and people fill them out. A report is compiled, and interpretations are made.

When measuring, one can still be blind to what actually should be measured. It would be more important to get people to say what is meaningful, rather than having them answer predetermined questions.

When people are asked something via a survey tool, it would be important that people could decide for themselves what is most meaningful to them. In traditional surveys there are several questions, and the respondent needs to assess each point separately – even though many of the points might not even matter to that respondent.

> **Take an example question: "How satisfied are you with the quality of the coffee?" If one-fifth of the respondents don't even drink coffee and they reply with a neutral grade, this distorts the results of the survey. A modern survey takes into account whether things are significant or not.**
>
> Mikko Koskinen, Siqni
> www.siqni.fi

If a survey asks about commission or bonus systems, you get data on those, but you can't deduce whether they are meaningful to the employees. An organisation features many scales of measurement that don't guide the organisation's culture of operations in the correct or desired direction. A classic example is to measure sales in one area of business operations, when you should actually be doing sales cooperation between different areas. Centralisation, mentioned in the previous chapter, distorts ways of thinking.

By developing measurement methods to measure only one thing, you get seemingly good results, which might not necessarily matter at all to people or to the entire organisation. At the same time, you end up influencing the organisation's culture and directing its operations via these methods of measurement. If the most important thing at work is to achieve good measurement results and work solely inside one's own box, cliques and internal competition arise. In reality you should be cooperating and building a culture to support the entire organisation's benefit.

A network's methods of measurement should encourage people to describe how the things that are most meaningful to them are fulfilled in everyday activities. The method of measuring the network can also not work well if it only measures the activities of a subset of the network.

In surveys, you can and should ask the members of the network whether they would recommend the activities of the network to others. A recommendation is always the outcome of how satisfied the members are with the activities of the network and how well the things they find meaningful are realised in the activities of the network.

When measuring you should focus on asking people what they feel is meaningful in their work, their hobby, or whatever other activity the network exists for. Furthermore you can ask how important they find this thing and how well it is realised in the network. This sort of measuring yields information on what influences people's actions and how much.

The measuring in itself produces new data, and this can be used to guide activities in a better direction. Often these kinds of measuring methods surprise you, because they can reveal completely new types of information.

If for instance the network measures the experiences of its members, you can get surprising results on why these people are members of the network.

If the measuring would have askec only about a predetermined list of things, you would only have gotten data cn those things. Via the measuring you now have understanding about why people are part of the network, and based on this information you can develop the activities of the network towards what the majority wants.

You can also measure customer experience based on the same idea. This way you can learn what customers actually find important and what influences them to choose their supplier. It comes as a full surprise to many supplier organisations when they find out what customers value. Usually the supplier's operations and sales have emphasized completely different things.

6.3 In a Network You Dare to Experiment

Networks can be best developed when everyone is kept up-to-date regarding things they are interested in. All information in the network should be open, so that anyone interested in development can deduce for themselves what influences what and how much.

People very interested in certain aspects of a network's activities – such as communication, surveying the potentials of AI, or legal matters – can if they so desire form a group that is responsible for that particular topic in the network. Because information is open and no one is delimited out, this activity can be developed in relation to the network as a whole.

Development and network activities do not have to be a Wild West: the network can have people responsible for specific areas, hierarchy, and other rules about how one can join various groups. It is an advantage to the network to have clear rules regarding how things can be influenced. It is even more important that these rules can be updated if necessary, and that the network features a strong culture of experimentation.

In other words, you don't have to implement every hare-brained and risky idea that just anyone has, but a well-rationalised and by-the-rules idea demands a chance to try it out.

Progress does not happen without experiments and accidents. A successful development usually requires a heap of failures in its wake. In a network you dare to try despite the risks, and due to the openness of information you can see the results quickly. Bad experimentations should of course not be continued, but learned from. This guides the activities of the network and the development of these activities in a new direction.

Progress should be measured, because otherwise the network's activities are not systematic and you can't deduce how well the development has succeeded. When measuring, you need to take note that you know what direction you want to develop activities in. If you want to purely serve the network and its members, you need to give the respondents the opportunity to tell you what they find important. If the network is to be developed in a direction chosen by a single person or a small group, it might be worth questioning why this is done.

For instance, an association formed around a hobby or interest should have its activities serve its members. The same is true for a company operating by community-led orientation based on principles of shared leadership. When the activities of a charity association are measured, you should also measure the results achieved. The same is true for a company where the board of directors determines what should be done. The latter examples aren't really networks as such, but rather organisations that have been given a predetermined purpose – even though people within them do operate in networks.

The Helsinki city library Oodi is a community-oriented organisation. The employees can plan and decide everything for themselves, but the purpose is to serve the citizens and lend books. Thus you need to ask the citizens, i.e.

the customers, what things they find meaningful. The sum of their and the employees' experiences tells how that organisation should be developed.

A network's purpose defines why, how, and in what direction it should be developed. If a network's point is to serve a given purpose, you should take into account every member's attitude towards this purpose and measure how important it is seen as. If a network serves an external entity, you need to find out what the external entity feels is meaningful.

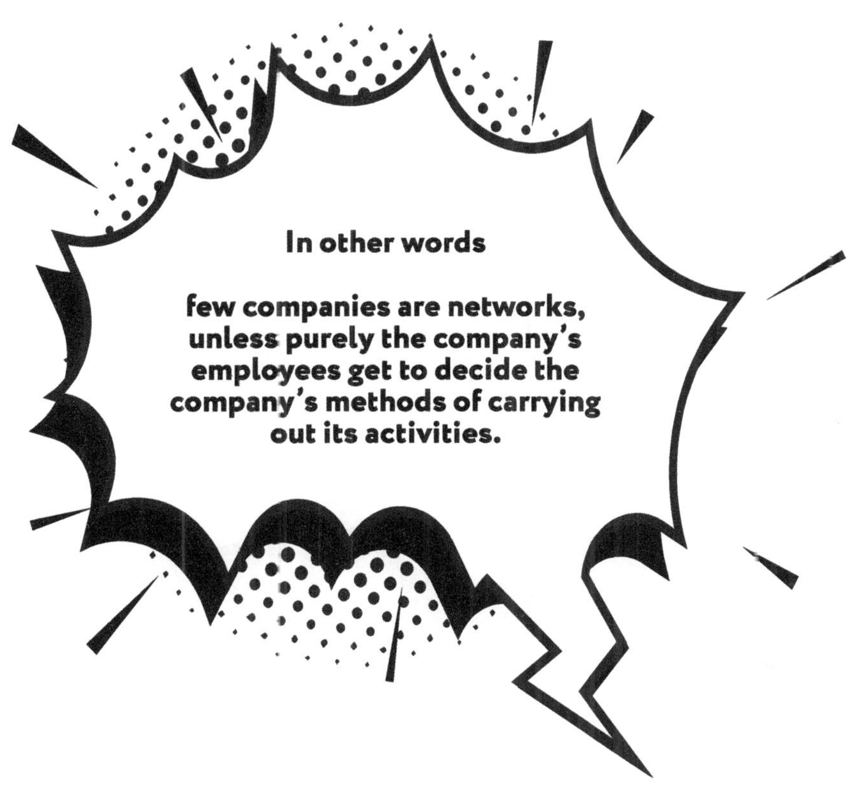

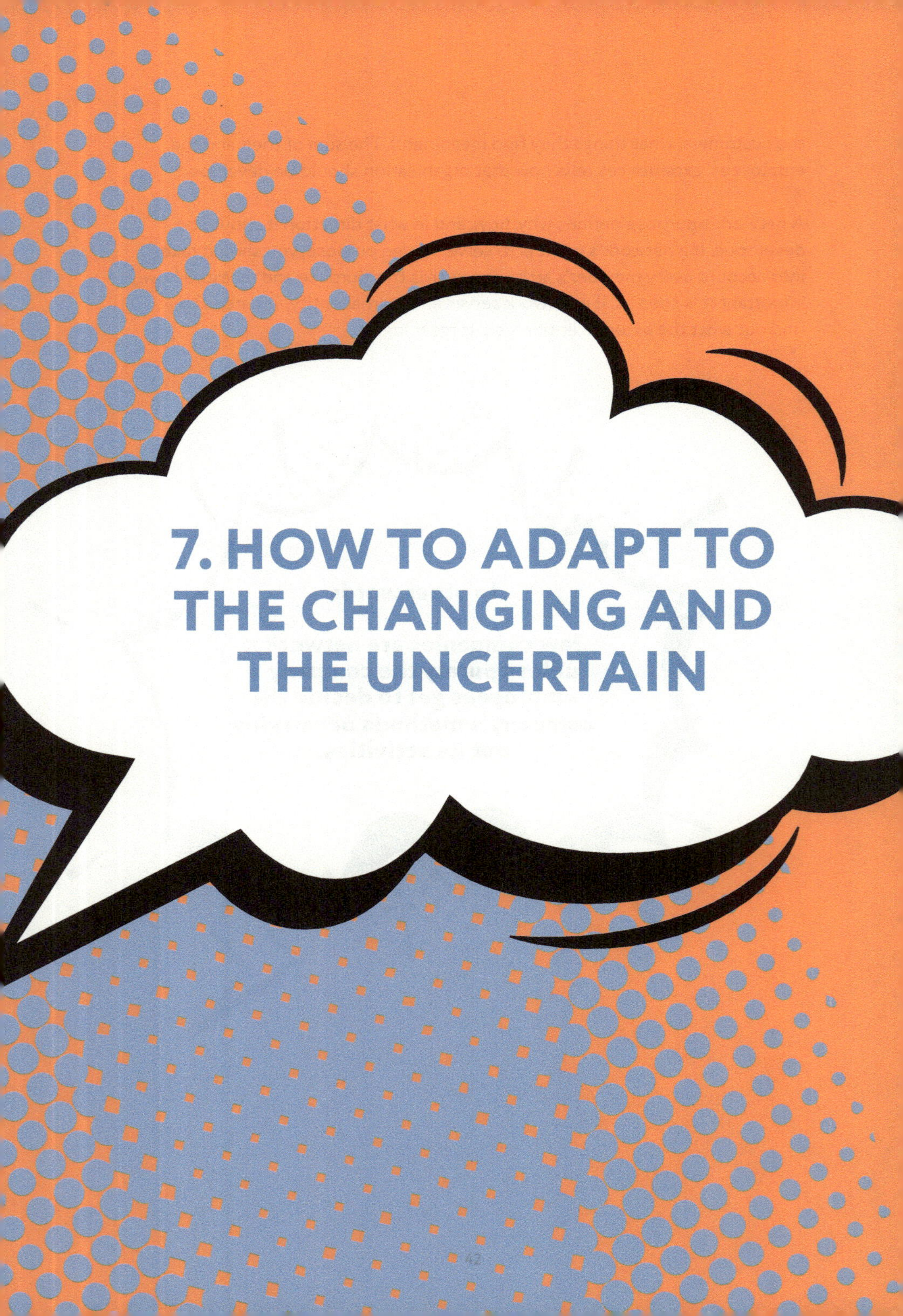

7. HOW TO ADAPT TO THE CHANGING AND THE UNCERTAIN

7.1 Agile Leadership

Agility means, as the name implies, activities where you can quickly react to various situations. A common misconception is that you don't have to document, note things down, or generally do a job properly when doing agile work. In work life people often say "let's do this agilely" and mean doing it without being systematic or without any framework.

In reality, agile work is done when various variables of the work aren't fixed.

Fixed or rigid work means that we know the schedule, the people who do the work, and the scope of the work, and if any of these change, we're in trouble: the work should be done faster, we're lacking doers, or the amount of work increases. Agility means that e.g. only two of these three variables are fixed. We have a schedule and the doers, but we can adjust the scope of the work. We have a schedule and the scope, but we can add more doers, or we have the scope of the job and the doers, but we can change the schedule.

Another aspect of agility is the potential to work at different times than others. Then work needs different task lists, from which people can check the things that have to be completed for the work or the project. When the priority of the tasks changes, we immediately update this on the list. When someone claims a task, this is also noted on the task list. When anyone looks at the task list, they immediately see where we are in terms of the work. We don't have to hold separate meetings for situation reports. The information and details about the tasks are noted onto this list as well, so that you don't have to look for the information from among e-mails or ask others for it.

Agility does not mean that meetings aren't held or that information couldn't be exchanged simultaneously. When you meet face-to-face, meetings are kept efficient and sensible. Each meeting has a clear point, and things are gone through according to the task list. If the matter being discussed isn't already on the task list, it is written down onto the list in the proper place. If the matter being discussed isn't related to an upcoming task, you could call into question why it's being discussed within the frame of this project or work.

Documentation of agile work is done via task lists. You can easily compile a traditional long-form document about completed jobs, from which you can find out what jobs have been completed and how. While doing the work the task list lives agilely. Only after the work or project is completed is the task list affixed in print and archived away in case of possible future follow-up projects.

7.2 Getting Away from the Constant Meeting Spiral

People tire of having their whole work day consist of meeting after meeting.
The day is made even heavier by the fact that the meetings are being held
online, and you have to sit in front of the computer. The constant meetings
don't leave any room for actual work. Work has to be done outside the meeting spiral, and the work day stretches into overtime. When you finally have a
few hours, you might find you're low on energy. People are used to this, even
though it doesn't have to be like this.

You should have time at work to develop things, to create new things, and to
focus on work itself. If a colleague needs your help, you need to have time
to help. Proverbial fires may pop up, or other types of urgent situations may
emerge, and you have to be able to react to them. Like in sports, you need a
lighter load and rest in order to have the strength to do the work. Weekends
aren't for recovering from work, but for your own personal life.

A constant spiral of meetings makes work inefficient. People are involved in
too many things if they have 40 hours per week of meetings. The organisation's culture is skewed if people have several different meeting invitations
simultaneously and they have to jump between them.

In a network you have to respect others' time, but you also have to clearly
express your need for help. The only way out of the constant meeting
spiral is asynchronous work model, i.e. working at different times. A natural
example of this is instant messaging services. Someone sends a message,
and you reply to it when it suits you. You share information when it fits you.
When problems are complicated, it's worth having a quick call, which requires some simultaneous work. In these the participants usually already know
what the topic of the conversation is, and can get right to the point.

Instant messaging services and chat conversations are useful for quick and
sudden "right now"-conversations, but poor for more detailed handling
of things. Thread-based applications – such as Facebook, LinkedIn, Slack,
Teams – are better for this, as then the topic stays within one thread, you
can link to a certain section later, and you can invite other people into the
thread. All conversations are available to everyone, but they're not forcibly
shoved onto anyone. Concerned parties are marked into the conversation
and they're expected replies from, and other interested parties may participate as well.

7.3 Managing Your Own Work

A person can't participate in the agile model and step out of the meeting spiral if they aren't able to manage their own work and time. It's difficult to start setting rules, boundaries, and schedules for yourself if for your whole life you've gotten used to someone else sorting these out for you. The traditional leadership culture and micromanagement in particular are someone else constantly telling you what you should be doing.

In a network everyone needs to be able to manage their own work – or at least be able to admit that they can't manage their own work. Then they should ask for help.

Within networks smaller groups are formed, in which the more dominant personalities gather around them people who want things more handed to them. This is natural and acceptable. This is how we naturally act. In networks it is, however, important to highlight this phenomenon so that people become aware of it. Things have to be said out loud, and you have to agree that regarding this topic we handle things this way.

As time passes, people will begin to want to define their own work themselves as well. The activities of the network are often such in nature, that some things are done together, but there are always things for everyone to do on their own. The members of the network have to be able to handle their own responsibilities and tasks before their next group meetings. If someone repeatedly shows up and declares that they've not done their tasks, they should be detached from the network. Why hang on to a freeloader?

In traditional leadership freeloading is enabled in many ways, and people rarely rat out their colleagues. When operating in a network, where everyone is equal and where everyone contributes, there isn't really much space given to freeloading. A talkative but lazy "cool person" can only coast on their personality for so long. Soon it will start to be clear to everyone who actually does the work and who doesn't. People will start having thoughts about why they should have to do more work than the freeloader.

Managing one's own work means a person's self-determination i.e. their ability to operate without external guidance. The self-determination theory presents three factors which influence a person's motivation.

-   *Autonomy means that the individual has power over and responsibility for their own work. For instance, even though you might get the profit target from elsewhere, you get to decide for yourself how to reach it. Autonomy is close to the concept of internal entrepreneurship.*

-   *Competence means that the work tasks challenge you and your whole knowledge base, beyond your regular professional knowledge. To challenge means constant chances for development. Competence does therefore not mean that you know how to do your job, but rather that the job itself challenges you and all your skills.*

-   *Relatedness means that the individual can identify themselves as part of a group that they see as important. Your own values match up with the company's values, and you feel pride in being part of a collective. Relatedness is often misinterpreted as there being a good vibe and team spirit at work.*

The more the factors presented here get stronger, the more self-determined a person is. You need self-determined people in a network. It is vital in a network that people can place their tasks in order of importance and manage the things that are their responsibility – and if they cannot do this, the problem should be reported to the others without delay.

7.4 Non-Simultaneous Work Pace

An asynchronous i.e. non-simultaneous work pace in practical terms means that we use information technology to communicate. Moving things along does not require agreeing about things in meetings where everyone is present at the same time.

A non-simultaneous work pace requires that the network members want to work efficiently and have the ability to manage their own work. When these assumptions are fulfilled, you can move to operating non-simultaneously.

This is our way of working.

- **We do not drown people in a constant torrent of meetings, but conversely you have to take part in conversations and be available.**

- **You should be able to manage your time so that you can complete the tasks that are your responsibility on time.**

- **You need to have the ability to ask for help, and you should announce ahead of time if you can't progress with some task.**

AGILE TASK MANAGEMENT

THIS IS WHAT PEOPLE THINK IT MEANS:

WHAT IT'S ACTUALLY ABOUT:

Agility's relationship to meetings – people think agility just means that you don't hold meetings. In reality it is about an efficient, asynchronous work model.

You don't get answers as quickly when working non-simultaneously, but in the larger picture, work progresses more efficiently. No one becomes a bottleneck due to their own schedule.

Work is done in small teams, and teams are created independently based on conversations and interests. People don't have to wait for permission to do things, because everyone has the power to do things. Motivation increases, because everyone feels that they can progress at their own pace and won't have to wait for others.

Putting things in order of importance is easier, because the things have already been gone through with those who are interested. The work is distributed among those who are interested, and people take things as their responsibilities. The areas of responsibility become clear, because meetings aren't cut short due to lack of time, and things aren't left up in the air. You can always find a responsible person for each thing: the person who feels they want to progress that thing.

In a network you teach everyone to follow a culture where you communicate efficiently, and both ask for and give feedback. The activities themselves give the members the tools for non-simultaneous communication while also teaching the usefulness of it. Everyone is directed to manage their own workload. Efficient communication doesn't take people's time and energy, but they learn to use their time sensibly and for the right things.

Through a non-simultaneous work pace you easily get things put into order of importance, and people get committed to the goals. People reserve enough time to complete the work tasks, and interest makes people prioritise these tasks. The final touch is to introduce a digital tool to help with task management, i.e. a task list/backlog. Everyone notes down their own tasks and what the status of each task is. This way all the members of the network are kept up-to-date about where other people's tasks are at – without having to hold meetings.

7.5 Reacting to Changing Situations

When the network has divided itself into small self-determined teams, uses task lists, and everyone manages their own activities, you can react quickly to changing situations. If the areas of responsibility and the tasks are clear, everyone can make necessary changes and communicate about them to others when it suits them. If the work in question is sizable, everyone in the network makes the necessary changes, after which a shared meeting is agreed on, where you discuss the details, goals, and the changed situations.

If the first step in the face of changing situations would be to arrange a meeting, much time would be wasted on finding a time suitable for everyone. Nothing can be done beforehand, but you have to wait for the meeting, where you still only go over the matter at hand. An agile network reacts independently to things, makes the changes, and then meets up to discuss the results and ponder further actions. A mutually agreed-upon path of action is quickly found during the meeting, because everyone has already pondered the issue for their own part, and time is not wasted on familiarising people with the issue.

If the calendar is full of meetings, there's no possibility to react to changes. And yet any of the booked meetings might get cancelled, as all sorts of small situations which require attending to will usually appear among the interest groups. A network does not operate in this kind of uncertain environment, because the network does not make long-term, rigid plans.

A network has a direction, goals, and an idea of whom the network's activities serve. The model and shape of the network is constantly shifting. The network adapts to its operational environment, and change is natural in the network.

In order to be able to react, it is important that the network has communication tools based on the latest technology, mutually agreed-on ways of communicating about things, and clear documentation or a clear task list, where the details and upcoming tasks are noted down. This way the network is not dependent on meetings and palavers. Every member of the network has the ability to control their own usage of time, and everyone can communicate about their work to others. Because of this the network is able to react quickly to changing situations and uphold all the agreed tasks and responsibilities.

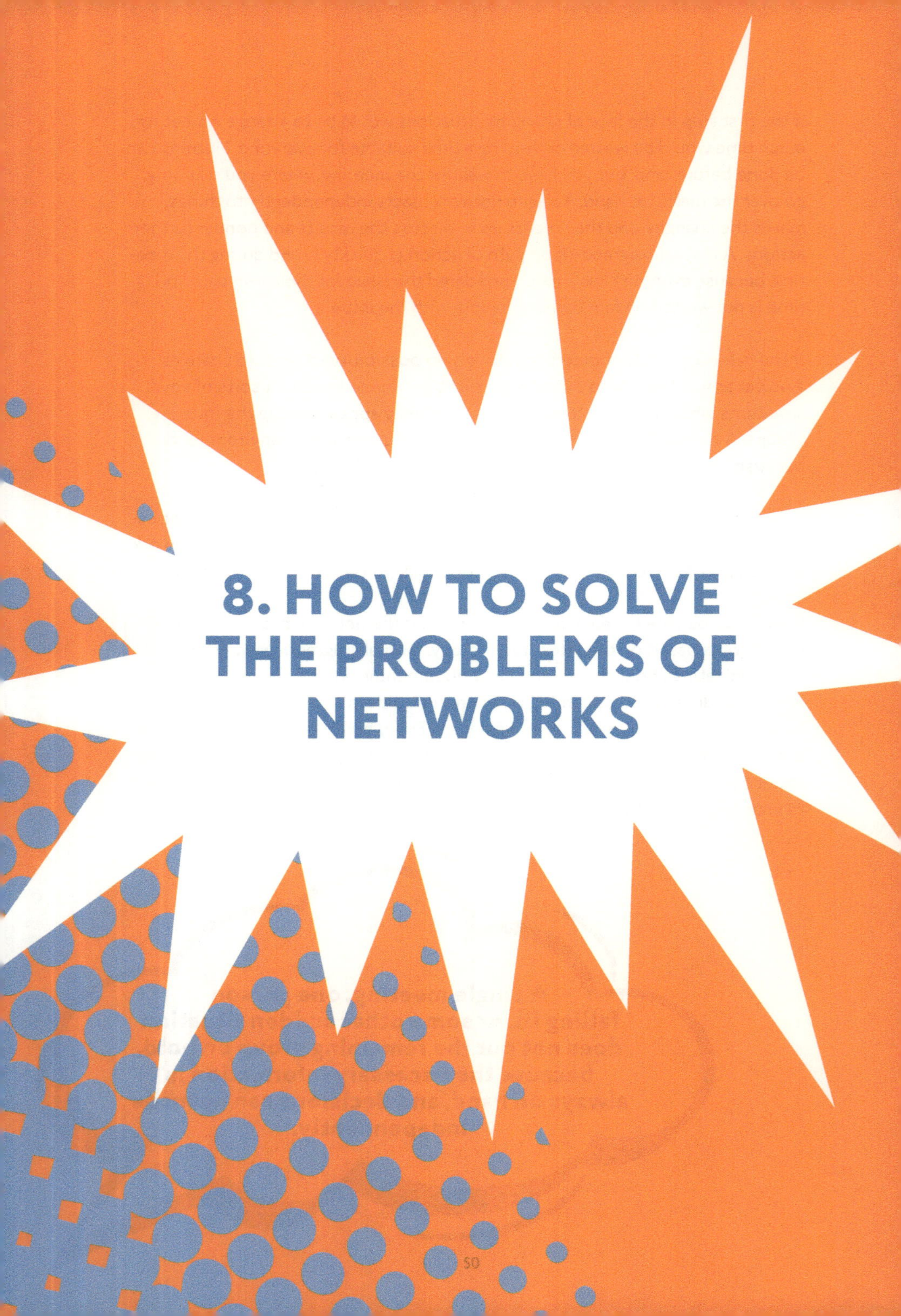

8. HOW TO SOLVE THE PROBLEMS OF NETWORKS

8.1 Uncontrollability is a Blessing and a Challenge

The activities of a network are based on parity and on no one nominally having power over another. Roles are created among the network members according to needs and situations. Positions are earned through competence, usefulness, and relations, and activities are based on a mutual goal or exchange.

Because of these reasons, a network cannot be controlled. No one can order others around on their own nor dictate how the network should function.

This uncontrollability gives everyone the opportunity to make decisions and to influence. The network also easily adapts to changing situations, as discussed in the previous chapter. On the other hand, it might become a difficulty for the network's activities that you can't predict what will happen.

Uncontrollability makes network leadership demanding, because you have to know the network, and you need to be able to trust it. You have to get the network to mutually agree on its ground rules, so that its activities can be guided in the same direction.

Mutually agreed-on rules don't always guarantee that every member of the network acts according to them. In professional or work life networks, you can usually count on agreed-on rules being followed, but when it comes to volunteer networks, people have a tendency to interpret and even disregard the rules. You often hear the saying "this is only a hobby". This is when you need to remind the members of the network about the shared rules and agreed-on practices.

Irrespective of whether the network's activities are hobby-based or not, no tasks is voluntary after you have promised to do it. By taking on the responsibility of a task you commit to this task, and you cannot leave it undone just because you're not getting monetary compensation for completing it. The people leading the network need to get the network's members to understand this.

The skill in network leadership lies in being able to use the network's uncontrollability to your advantage. Because there is no hierarchy, everyone can influence the network.

There is the risk that rules might get interpreted or circumvented for someone's personal gain. One's own gain might be disguised as the network's gain. The various parts of the network are uncontrollable in terms of the whole. On the other hand it's good that the network can be controlled according to multiple different goals.

Clarifying, developing and changing the network's goals is the key to whether its uncontrollability is a benefit or a hindrance. The network should serve a certain purpose, and its meaning directly influences how the members of the network operate. In this book the purpose of a network is discussed more in chapter 6.3, "In a Network You Dare to Experiment".

If a network's members suddenly want to do something completely different, and they feel the purpose of the network's activities has changed, the network is from one perspective uncontrollable, but from another perspective it is agile and adaptable.

8.2 Should All Problems Be Avoided?

A network is based on people's desires to do things together. If you try to avoid conflicts, you return back to traditional leadership cultures and stop functioning like a network. It's permitted to show emotions in a network, and

Whenever people are involved, there will always be conflicts. A more serious problem would be if people didn't say what they thought or wanted, and what they found lacking.

you should communicate to others about how you as an individual want to be treated.

Avoiding conflicts is like suppressing emotions and frustrations. On the other hand, the network's activities aren't meant to be anyone's personal therapy nor trauma management.

You should not avoid problems in networks, but rather you should be able to defuse such issues, so that dealing with them does not completely prevent the network's activities.

A community-oriented network should by itself define how conflicts are handled. One problem might be that the activities of the network aren't necessarily very close-knit, and it's hard to find time nor anyone willing to handle conflicts. The more close-knit the activities of the network are, the better people are at speaking up about problems and dealing with them.

If bringing up a problem causes an interruption in the activities, you could always ask whether the problem can be dealt with later. This way the network member feels that they are listened to, but they are then also able to temporarily let go of the issue. Sometimes the real cause of the conflict was tiredness, being in a hurry, or a poor night's sleep, and later on things might look quite different. Conflicts are difficult to resolve in a stressful situation or if everyone is already in a bad mood. A conflict can be resolved productively when the initial situation is more pleasant for everyone.

The most common feeling that causes problems is frustration. A person feels they are unfit for the situation, and that it's impossible to solve things amiably. The underlying reason might be a negative emotion from their childhood, which reflects upon the setbacks in the activities of the network. The emotion might arise from the person not having understood the meaning of the task, or that they feel the task was given to the wrong person. With frustration a person's behaviour becomes more cynical, and a conflict begins to dawn ahead.

An incident that appears small from an outside perspective might cause a large swell of emotion in a person. It's impossible to know what size of issues causes emotional turmoil for each person.

In a network it is important to regularly return to what you've promised. If you make promises in the network that you don't keep, a new problem arises: lack of trust. This kind of problem needs to be brought up, because the network itself is based on trust and exchange.

Trust creates a desire in people to help others and do their part towards a shared goal. The motivation to work in a network disappears if problems cannot be brought up.

8.3 Recovering From Conflicts

Sometimes you have to get a chance to talk about things and "let off steam". On the other hand, a person who hasn't been trained in dealing with emotions or who isn't in touch with their own emotional life can't necessarily help others with unpacking their emotional load. This sort of person might interpret conversations with others too concretely and draw the wrong conclusions about a worker's motivations.

Usually you "let off steam" during breaks and create unofficial peer support. In remote working the opportunities for these situations are diminished, and the network's members are more responsible for their own well-being. People should understand that the choice to stay home moves the responsibility for these things to themselves, because the network cannot as easily offer opportunities for peer support remotely as it might on-location.

Remote activities mean that the responsibility to seek support for one's work sits more with the network members themselves. On-location the work community would notice during shared meetings e.g. a person's coping problems or excessive stress. Many people don't consider this when they want to save on time and comfort. Is remote working worth the trouble of isolation, and will it come with an expensive trade-off?

If you can't unpack the emotional load, it will usually come out at the wrong time and place. Others can manage more pressure, others less, some can do it for weeks, others for years. Before long the emotional load will have effects on everyone's work, motivation, and health. The importance of recognising these sorts of things becomes emphasised in network activities, and it is an important skill to be able to ask for help.

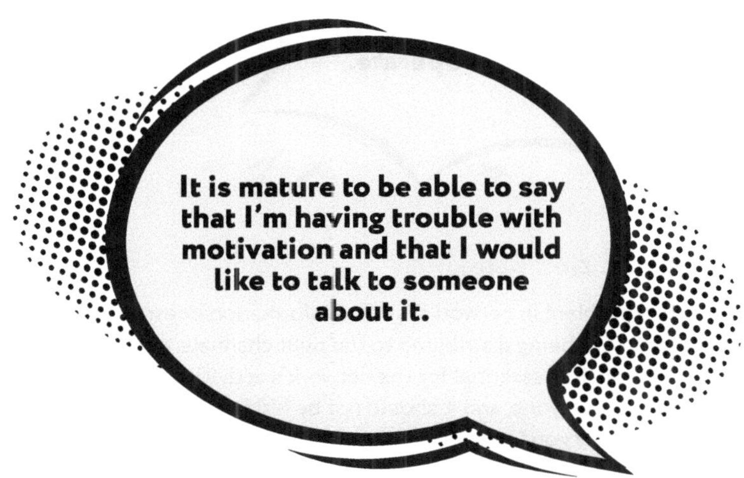

their emotions. It is the duty of experienced people to lead by example and show how to act in various situations. It's also good to go through with the members of the network how each person behaves in various extremes of emotional states, and how they would like to be treated in such situations.

Emotional matters should be discussed more often. You can't get stuck on them, and the network's activities should not be anyone's personal therapy sessions. Recovering from conflicts does however require discussion and guidelines.

By going over in advance different situations, you can teach people how to recover from conflicts. The network can write down common guidelines, just as with other things. These guidelines help, but when there's a situation in progress, you always need someone to remind people of these guidelines. Experienced or trained people can guide people in recovering from conflicts. Their job is to build ground rules for conflict recovery in the network.

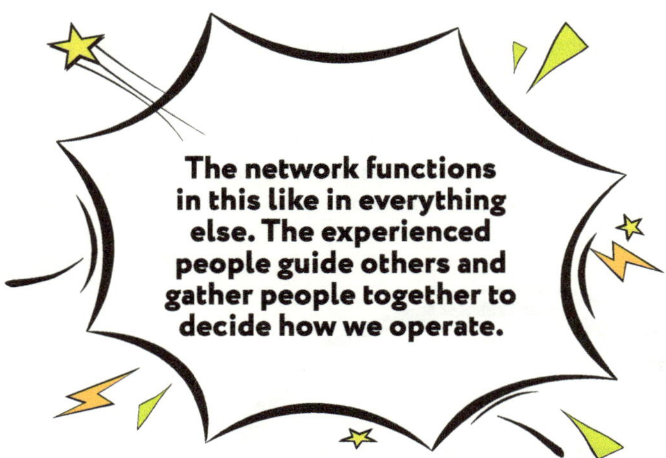

8.4 Information Blackouts

The greatest problem in networks is when information doesn't flow. Information is not being distributed to the right channels, or it piles up behind one person. It is essential for the network's activities that information is accessible to everyone, and it should not be hidden or concealed except with exceptionally good reason.

If information isn't accessible to everyone, activities are interrupted. When activities are interrupted, it might take a long time to start it back up. Usually an information blackout causes much more problems than just the moment when information is not available.

Some people assume that they can leave a task unfinished until someone inquires about it. "They'll ask, if they're interested." The people whom others request information from might feel that they don't need to pre-emptively share the information, but that they should instead wait for others to activate themselves. In professional contexts people are well-versed in inquiring for information and taking initiative in solving problems, but this is not always the case.

In volunteer activities and especially concerning unpleasant tasks an information blackout might easily cause the entire task to be left unfinished. In many situations people become more stupid than they really are, and might

If there is no information available, the doers will vanish at the first sight of an unclear situation, claiming they did not know what to do.

convince themselves they don't have to finish this task right now. People are skilled at convincing themselves to skip work tasks. When they've sold themselves on the idea, it's easy to justify themselves when others ask, throwing their hands in the air and saying they couldn't do anything about it.

Persistence and perseverance combined with compassion and determination are in a key role when you want to lead a network and its information flow. A person who manages to call and ask politely will ultimately get the information they seek. Seeking information, asking, and guiding others requires patience and a friendly attitude.

Sharing information should be made as easy as possible, and the people who shared the information should be left with the feeling that they were important.

Sometimes you might end up in a situation where information has to be gathered together or you have to get other people to make decisions together. In these situations it's good to remind people of the shared destination and goal, and motivate people to make the decision and gather the information. This sort of network leader quickly gets a good reputation for being able to make things happen. Leading a network is guiding people to work together and share information.

Through technology the sharing of information is easy. You need discussion platforms, and you need to teach the network members to share information via the proper channels or in the shared discussions, not just one-on-one, so that information-seeking does not become detective work, but the information is more easily found e.g. via search functions.

People have a tendency to send messages directly. Some don't want to bother people other than the recipient, some are ashamed of public discussions – there are many reasons. In a network you have to repeatedly remind and encourage people to make even incomplete information accessible to others. This way those interested can join the conversation, and an eager doer's motivation to do the task doesn't get cut short due to information not being available.

- *Information being available does not mean that all information should be pushed at everyone.*

- *Information should not be shared via e-mail.*

- *Shared discussion groups, e.g. WhatsApp chats, are not the best channel for sharing information.*

The best way to share information are discussion-based tools, such as Teams, Slack, Facebook, LinkedIn or others, where the conversation around one topic stays in one place, you can reference it with a link afterwards, and it is accessible via a search function.

The more professional the network is, the better the tools. Usually leisure time networks use social media and free tools, because there isn't money for better. In professional, work-oriented networks you see the benefits of paid tools, and such tools are invested in, because they save time and makes communicating more comfortable.

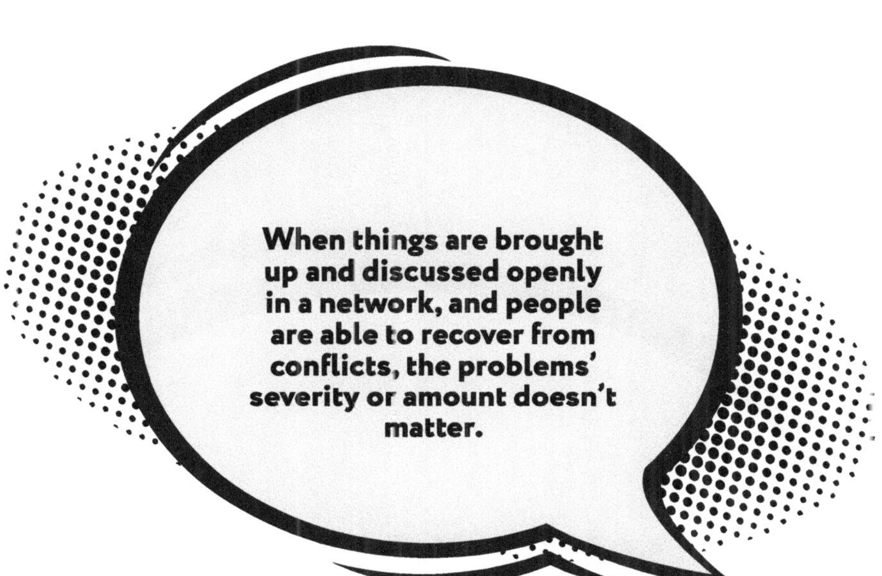
When things are brought
up and discussed openly
in a network, and people
are able to recover from
conflicts, the problems'
severity or amount doesn't
matter.

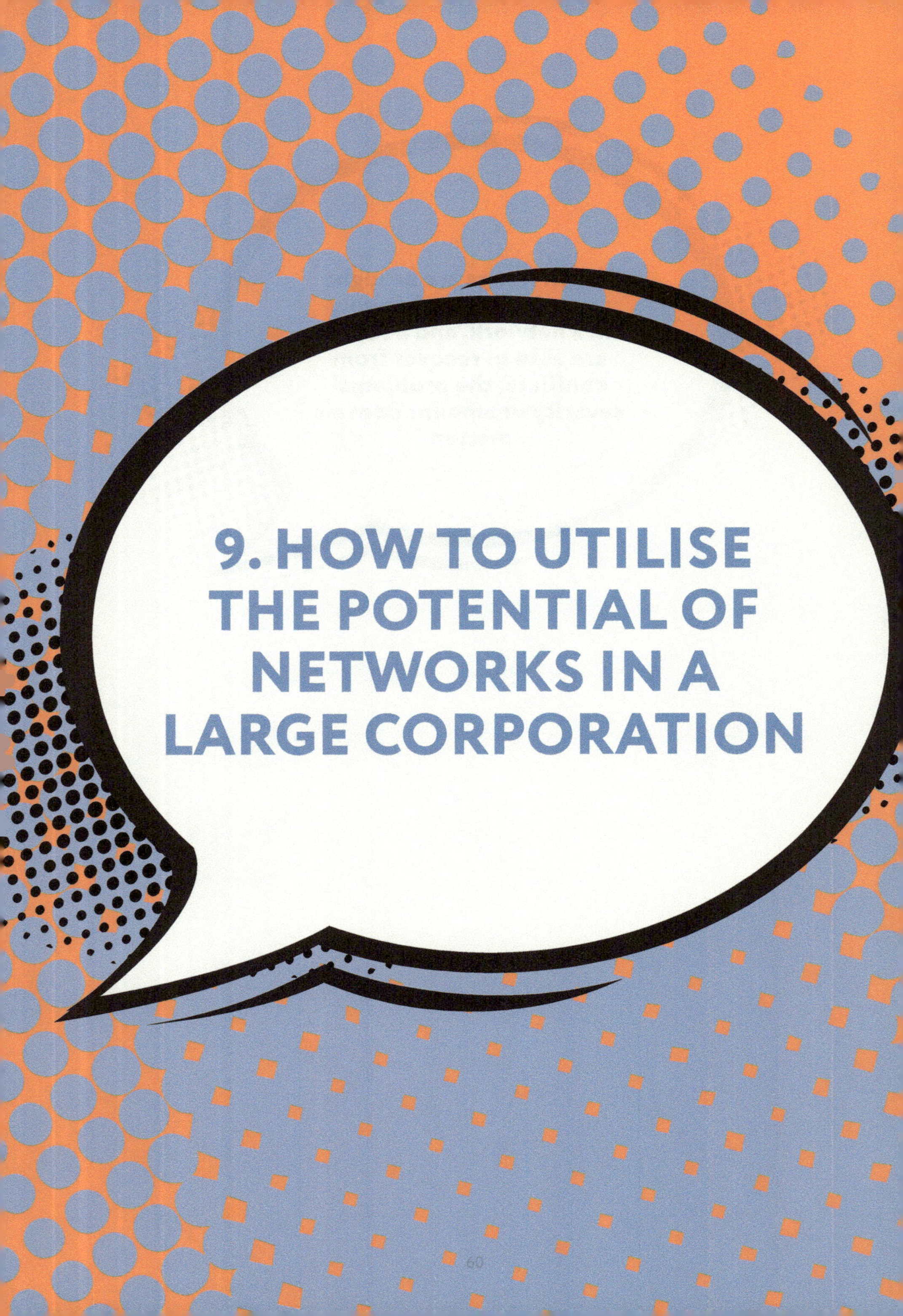

9. HOW TO UTILISE THE POTENTIAL OF NETWORKS IN A LARGE CORPORATION

9.1 Distinguish Pleasing From Manipulating

In large organisations there is a lot of hierarchy, i.e. supervisors and their supervisors, and several different departments, units, and teams. Even though the organisational structure is usually rigid and pyramid-like, in truth work happens in networks, which are based on friendship, shared interests, projects, or past work.

When there are a lot of people involved, you can't know everyone personally. A large amount of people includes a lot of different people, including those who want to advance things through manipulation.

In the beginning of the book there was a chapter about pleasing. It's not always possible to distinguish manipulation from pleasing. In a corporation you can recognise a manipulator from the fact that even though they are pleasant, smile at you and phrase things as a request, you actually don't have a choice about it. These kinds of people pretend to be polite and everybody's friend, but they are actually serving their own interests, and they are unscrupulous. A manipulative person will help you, but when an opportunity presents itself they will demand you return the favour, they will steal a pleasant task from you, take credit for your work, make you feel guilty about their mistakes, or just make you work at the limits of your ability to cope.

If you speak up against this kind of person, they will probably convince you that they are acting for the benefit of a) the organisation, b) the team, c) both of you, or d) you personally. You'll feel embarrassed about having felt mistreated. The manipulative person can do this knowingly or unknowingly. Some people have adopted the culture of a large corporation and believe that this is the correct way to act, because everybody else acts this way.

It is up to each of us individually whether to keep working in an unpleasant organisation. If you often feel bad and you feel the organisation's way of operating is wrong, there's no use blaming others and the company culture. Everyone has the opportunity to change jobs or organisations. Another option is to endure the company culture and find your own methods of persevering.

It is difficult to say whether manipulation is always wrong. If you want to enrich the culture of an organisation, you may have to do it by the organisation's rules in order to get the position you desire. It is up to you to decide for yourself about the ethical questions of when you'd be crossing the line and pursuing your own interests, and when you're just tilting at windmills on their own terms. It's always worth considering your own actions, and whether you would like to be treated the same way. You should also be merciful to yourself. We can all change or change our ways, irrespective of our pasts.

9.2 The Curtain of Acting Can Be Dropped

In large corporations people are usually engaging in a role: they are acting differently from how they are feeling inside. When the leadership culture is traditional and hierarchical, it's not normal to show vulnerability and open up your inner self. Everyone has a public-facing work role that they carry with them.

Inside the organisation in their own networks people are more themselves. The smaller and more familiar the network, the less people perform a role i.e. pretend to be something they're not.

All of us have different roles at work, at home, in hobbies, and with different people. There is nothing wrong with such roles, if they don't consume energy from the person. When carrying out a role starts to weigh, tire, and begins to make you feel bad, it's worth pondering how the role could be lightened. Is it possible to direct more work to be done in a safe network? When you're exhausted and tired, often the most radical and quickest solution seems the most appropriate.

When in emotional turmoil people's roles can drop, and an altogether different role of the person takes over. The subconscious is then trying to resolve the problem by exacerbating the situation. As a consequence, the person gets to be more themselves, they get given space around them or others ask for a change of surroundings for them.

Many feel that they are forced to act a certain way or act out a certain persona in order to succeed at work or hold on to their place in

We all have many different roles, between which we balance.

the corporation. Sometimes this may be true, but the curtain of acting can also be gradually dropped. All of us have the opportunity to change our own behaviour. The best way is to make small changes at a time, so that others and you yourself can get used to the changes over time. It's worth feeling the situation and checking how others react when you do things differently. It's also recommended to get someone to talk about these things with, such as a colleague, an HR representative, or an occupational psychologist.

Generally people-oriented people don't get stressed-out about roles, and easily blend into a culture of acting. For them the company of others and small changes in their own behaviour doesn't matter. They might feel that the role is the small spark of fun that makes work interesting. On the other hand matter-oriented people can feel that the company of others consumes their energy and makes work exhausting. Some of them focus solely on matters and hide behind their professional role, where emotions aren't shown and you only ever focus on the matter at hand, and don't chat any further.

In corporations it's worth creating interpersonal relations and learning how people are when they drop their roles. Beneath there might be a completely different person than what you'd imagined. Others can be determined and tough on the outside, but are actually shy and sensitive inside. Some might seem quiet and sensitive, but actually be determined and efficient inside. The larger the organisation, the more people often act like something they're not.

9.3 Quiet Leadership

Quiet leadership means that it's not a person's title or position in the organisation that gives them power, but that they lead in some other way. A quiet
leader can be a well-liked person who is fair, upstanding, and respected.
When they ask about or ponder something, others follow their opinion, and
the supervisors want to do as they instruct.

A quiet leader can also be a good performer and manipulator. A person with
narcissistic traits can hold others in a tight grip and spin even a large circle
of people in the way they want. They might talk about others behind their
backs, create conflicts, and intimidate others to get what they want. This
kind of people should be avoided and kept at a distance, because they are
not your friends, even though they pretend to be. They will betray your trust
when the going gets tough.

People with poor self-esteem get annoyed by quiet leaders. It bothers them
that someone else takes authority away from them and throws a spanner in
their works. They will let it be in front of others, but they are pondering to
themselves about how to take the authority away from the quiet leaders.
They should be pondering why the quiet leaders have attained their position,
instead of getting involved in a power struggle.

Supervisors who are comfortable with themselves will see the quiet leaders
as good contributors in the organisation. They understand that with the help
of quiet leaders, things can be achieved quicker and more efficiently than
in the traditional way. These supervisors aren't afraid of heroes or birds of
ill omen, but are able to handle them so that they feel that they are valuable
members of the working community.

It's important for the operations of a network that people have an idea of
how the network functions in a hierarchical corporation. Network leadership
does not mean that you need a quiet leader or a supervisor, but the network
also does not exclude these roles.

A network leader is able to recognise acting and manipulation, and can guide
people in the right direction. A network leader protects their friends and
colleagues in the corporation, and keeps other people satisfied.

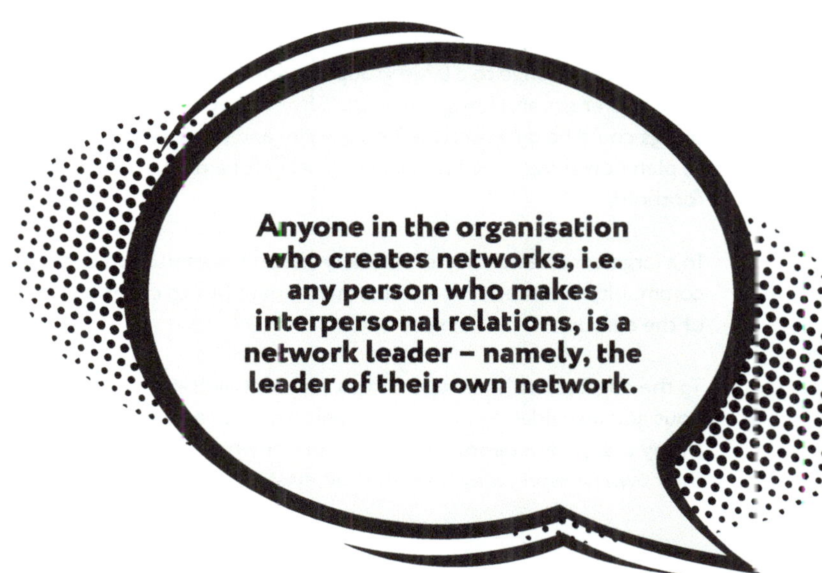

9.4 Secret Organisations

A secret organisation can develop inside a corporation, organisation, or network. A secret organisation means a group of people who share the same values and goals, but who don't directly think of themselves as a group.

One good example is people who like to party. In time they recognise each other and start gathering at parties. Another example could be people grouping up around some hobby. A secret organisation doesn't try to remain secret, but dismisses its own existence and doesn't think of the group as "us".

In a community-oriented leadership culture you try to bring up different interests, hobbies, and desires. These are made public, and people are given the freedom to be what they are. At the same time, secret organisations get unearthed.

A network functions like a community-led organisation. Networks have always existed, and modern leadership has not invented anything new to add to them. By talking about community-led orientation we try to bring up natural ways for people to function and make them into new working life customs.

Bringing the change to a large group of people always requires that you first raise awareness and bring things up. After this you start talking about how things could be differently. When the aim and the idea get support, you start to plan how things need to change in order for a new kind of culture to get a foothold.

In a large corporation there is usually a secret organisation dedicated to community-oriented leadership, which would like to change the operations of the corporation to be more open.

To the corporation's management, a secret organisation might appear rebellious and intimidating. A secret organisation can actually be harmful as well. In any case, these people have a role under which they work, and when in their own network, they take off their mask.

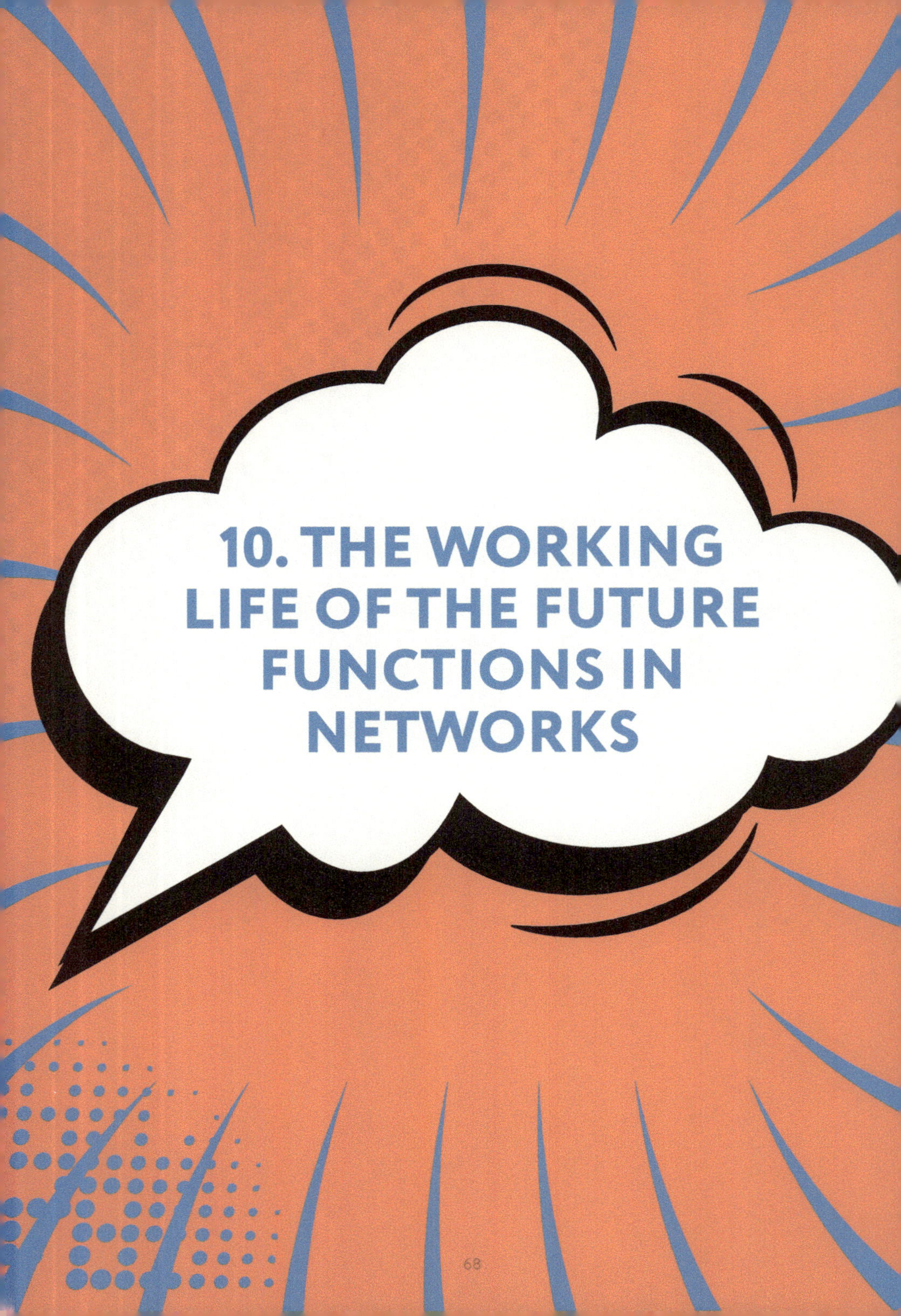
10. THE WORKING LIFE OF THE FUTURE FUNCTIONS IN NETWORKS

Networks contain a great power, because they serve people's deepest desires and wishes. Networks organise themselves in a natural way for people, and they are led by people who have the skill to lead others.

The working life of the future functions more like networks, but the change is slow. The majority of people don't think about these things, but act like they always have, because it's easy and safe, familiar.

A network can change things more efficiently than a traditional organisation. A network doesn't have boundaries or limitations, because a network can be created inside another network or organisation. A network can stretch across the borders of multiple networks or organisations. A network favours its own, and within the network sharing thoughts and ideas is easy. Change is always enacted with networks, not by commanding.

A network is based on the motivation and desire to do things. A network's activities usually give people a good feeling and the desire for more. A network gives people meaning and a sense of belonging to something important: network membership feeds people's self-determination and sense of self-worth. A network is a versatile – and when misused, dangerous – way of influencing people.

Networks will always exist, and leading them is influencing people. The skills for leading a network are within all of our grasp. Some of us may already possess many of the attributes of a network leader, but anyone can learn these skills.

Every one of us belongs to several networks and directs them through their own actions. By paying attention to how a network functions and how you function, you can achieve a lot.

The biggest reason to lead a network is usually the sense of well-being you get. This can be done for the wrong or the right reasons. A network can be led wrong or right. A person can manipulate and pretend, or be fair and encourage others. No one way is inherently better, if you purely look at network leadership and not what's right. Different things are right and wrong in different cultures. It's impossible to say that this thing is right in this network, when it's wrong in that other one.

The opportunity of networks for each of us is to teach us about ourselves, how we treat others. If we cannot become part of a network, we've done something wrong or the network is the wrong one for us. As long as we don't dare to open our eyes, we blame others for us being left outside of networks, and we don't see the flaws in ourselves. We can also be blinded by some desire or dream, and we might think we want to be part of a network which isn't really a good fit for us.

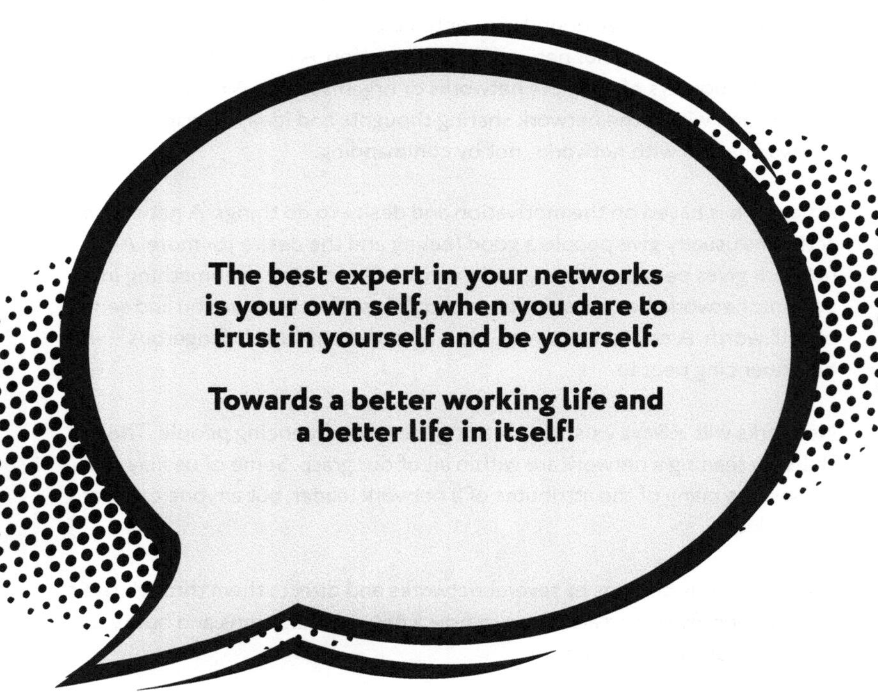

11. CLOSING WORDS

Thanks to the Youth Chamber of Commerce, which is my life's biggest network and teacher on community-led orientation, motivation, and networking. I've learned a lot about myself and about how to function with different people in various different situations. When a network is based on voluntariness, you have to learn to lead yourself, your own motivation, so that you can lead others.

During my life I have learned a lot by doing and by reading. The biggest lesson comes from doing and working with different people – different than yourself. Networks exist wherever we interact with other people.

Growing up in the middle of the woods without nearby friends, I always had to make an effort to belong to various networks.

Since I was little I've learned that you have to be yourself and do the things that you feel are important to yourself. Networks are formed around that which I am, and through this I can lead them. You should also remember to treat others the way you want yourself to be treated. This way you will find yourself in such networks that bring you energy and joy in your life.

I hope this book opened your eyes about how to function in networks, and how they can be led. Leading a network means getting to know others, guiding others, and helping others in different situations. With these lessons you can enter any network, observe its activities, and shape the network in the way you want.

Great power brings great responsibility.

Networks contain a truly great power. It's worth upholding that responsibility and teaching it onwards to others.

La Capucinière
ou le bijou enlevé à la course (1780)

Pierre-François Tissot

Chez les Marchands de Nouveautés, Paris, 1820

© 2023 SHS Editions
Le portail des sciences humaines et sociales
Illustration de couverture : © domaine public
Edition : SHS éditions (Hérault, 34)
Contact : infos@culturea.fr
Imprimé en Allemagne par Books on Demand
In de Tarpen 42, Norderstedt.
Design typographique : Derek Murphy
Layout : Reedsy (https://reedsy.com/)
ISBN : 9791041914555
Dépôt légal : Avril 2023

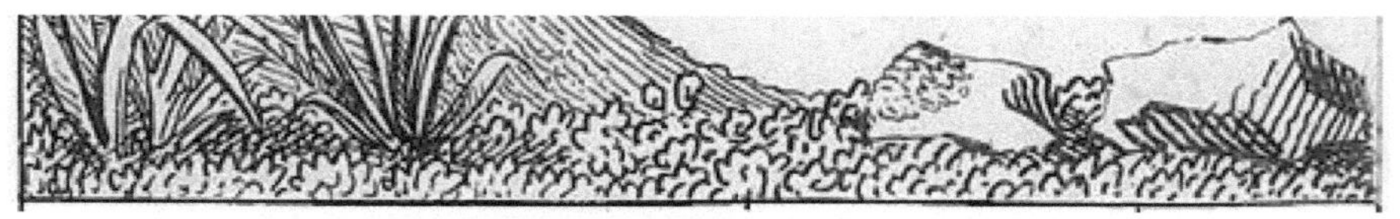

Les Plaisirs de l'ancien régime, et de tous les âges,
Illustration.

La Capucinière

Bandeau

A

AGLAURE.

Toi qui sais allier une gaîté charmante
    Aux tendres sentimens du cœur ;
Toi qui ne fus jamais ni prude, ni pédante,
Qui te plais à sourire aux bons mots d'un conteur,
    Qui lis Parny, Lafontaine, Voltaire,
Et n'en prises pas moins les écrits d'un docteur ;
    De cet enfant d'une muse légère,
      Reçois l'hommage volontaire.
D'avance, je m'attends que de tristes censeurs
    S'en prévaudront pour critiquer mes mœurs :

3

Ils vont tonner ; dans leur colère,
Ils traiteront de blasphèmes affreux,
Jusques aux moindres mots de ma *Capucinière* ;
Mais au lieu d'applaudir à ce zèle pieux,
L'homme sage, avec nous, rira de leur folie :

Il sait qu'on peut fort bien, sans offenser les Dieux,
Se permettre parfois une plaisanterie,
Sur les prêtres, les Saints, et même sur Marie.
Il sait encor qu'on peut avoir des mœurs,
Et peindre ceux qui n'en ont guères,
Défions-nous de ces frondeurs :
Sous les dehors les plus austères,
Ils cachent le cœur le plus faux.
Défions-nous de ces belles mystiques
Qui, se pâmant sur des reliques,
De leur sexe ont tous les défauts,
Et nulles vertus en partage.
Au seul aspect d'un livre, on les voit en fureur ;
Elles voudraient brûler et l'auteur et l'ouvrage ;
Mais, tête-à-tête avec leur directeur,
Au dieu d'Amour elles rendent hommage,
Et bénissent cent fois et l'ouvrage et l'auteur.

AVANT-PROPOS.

Nous ne dirons pas comment cette bluette est tombée entre nos mains ; le public est, sans doute, fort peu curieux de le savoir. Il nous paraît également inutile de lui en faire connaître l'auteur. Si elle est assez heureuse pour amuser, son nom n'ajoutera rien au plaisir qu'elle procurera. Si, au contraire, elle ennuie, raison de plus pour que l'auteur reste inconnu.

En supposant que des plaisanteries dussent être prises au sérieux, nous conviendrons que cet ouvrage pourrait, à la rigueur, être taxé de renfermer quelques traits hardis et quelques peintures un peu libres ; mais alors nous demanderons ce qu'a donc avancé l'auteur de la *Capucinière,* que les écrivains les plus célèbres du dix-huitième siècle n'aient dit avant lui ? Ouvrons les œuvres de Voltaire, de Diderot, de Boulanger, d'Helvétius, de l'abbé Raynal, &c., nous y trouverons, à chaque page, le ridicule semé à pleines mains sur notre religion, qui, d'après M. Geoffroy lui-même, ne vaut pas mieux que celle des peuples les plus barbares[1]. Leurs écrits d'ailleurs

l'attaquent ouvertement ; au lieu que notre auteur n'en a
parlé que par occasion, et parce qu'elle tenait à son sujet.
Ce n'est qu'aux couvens qu'il paraît en vouloir. Eh ! n'est-il
donc pas reconnu maintenant que le culte catholique peut
très-bien se passer de moines, de capucins, de nonnes, de
cloîtres en un mot ? Mais les prêtres et les bigots, intéressés
à arrêter la propagation de cette vérité, s'emporteront
toujours contre l'homme courageux qui dénoncera ces
repaires du vice, ou de véritables animaux se réunissent

> Pour s'engraisser et vivre à nos dépens.

Il est un reproche plus fondé en apparence, qu'on
pourrait adresser à notre auteur. Je veux parler des mœurs
qu'il n'a pas assez respectées, dira-t-on. Nous ne pensons
pas qu'en chantant des capucins, il ait eu la prétention de
faire un cours de morale. Quoi qu'il en soit, son ouvrage
n'en est pas entièrement dépourvu, et il nous serait facile de
le prouver. Mais examinons si ceux qui ont écrit dans le
même genre, ont été plus réservés que lui. Sans parler des
productions des anciens, et en nous restreignant à celles des
écrivains de nos jours et de notre pays, nous verrons que
l'auteur de la *Capucinière* a été bien moins libre que ses
maîtres.

Dans la *Pucelle*, Jeanne aux prises avec le Muletier et
Grisbourdon, aux prises avec son âne brûlant d'amour pour
elle ; dans *la Guerre des Dieux*, la Parodie de la Passion de
Notre Seigneur, la Chapelle des Claques, les Exploits de

Priape et de ses Satyres ; dans *les Bijoux indiscrets* et dans *Parapilla*, les Aveux des Bijoux, les Fredaines de Parapilla ; enfin dans *les Contes de Lafontaine*, les Trois Commères, le Berceau, &c. ; toutes ces scènes ne sont-elles pas bien plus indécentes que celles de la *Capucinière* ? Cependant ces ouvrages se vendent publiquement et par-tout.

Au surplus, si notre auteur a présenté quelques tableaux trop libres parfois, du moins ses expressions sont toujours chastes ; et, à l'exception de deux ou trois mots, qu'il lui aurait été impossible de ne pas employer, tels que *pucelage* et *pucelle*, sa *Capucinière* n'en offre aucun qui ne dût être reçu dans la meilleure société. Or, le bon homme a dit :

> Quand le mot est bien trouvé,
> Le sexe, en sa faveur, à la chose pardonne.
> Ce n'est plus elle alors, c'est elle encor pourtant :
> Vous ne faites rougir personne,
> Et tout le monde vous entend.

Sommaires des cinq Chants.

Chant Ier   *Pl. II.*

Les Plaisirs de l'ancien régime, et de tous les âges,
Illustration.

> *Tandis qu'ainsi la bataille s'engage*
> *Le grand François…*

Bandeau

LA
CAPUCINIÈRE,
POÈME

CHANT PREMIER

Dans l'âge heureux où l'aimable Folie,
Prenant pitié du pauvre genre humain,
Pour adoucir son funeste destin,
Sème de fleurs le chemin de la vie,
Le dieu des cœurs m'inspira l'art des vers :
Il me l'apprit ; et par reconnaissance,
J'ai fait serment de vieillir dans ses fers.

Célie, Ismée, Euphrosine et Constance,
Ont tour à tour couronné leur vainqueur.
Bientôt après, la séduisante Aglaure
Me fit ouïr l'aveu le plus flatteur ;

Et dans mes bras, ivre de mon bonheur,
Elle jura que le dieu que j'adore
Serait aussi le seul dieu de son cœur.

    Amour, tu vois si je te suis fidèle !
Quoique, toujours, volant de belle en belle,
Je n'ai jamais respiré que pour toi ;
Mais c'est trop peu pour ce que je te doi :
Assez long-temps j'ai gardé le silence ;
Il faut le rompre, il faut, en vers pieux,
Dire tes lois, célébrer ta puissance,
En transmettant à nos derniers neveux,
Un fait plaisant, mais un peu scandaleux.

    Pour raconter une si belle histoire,
Amour, Amour, soutiens ma faible voix,
Viens m'inspirer, il y va de ta gloire.
D'autres, sans nous, vanteront les exploits
Des conquérans chéris de la victoire :
Je ne veux pas de si fameux héros ;
Je dirais mal leurs glorieux travaux ;
Ma muse est tendre et point du tout guerrière.

Mais s'il suffit de brûler de tes feux
Pour essayer, sur cette autre matière,

Quatre ou cinq chants à demi-sérieux,
Amour, je puis entrer dans la carrière,
Plus d'une fois je t'ai dû mon bonheur ;
D'Aglaure encor je possède le cœur,
Et chaque jour, alors que la nuit sombre
Descend des cieux et nous laisse dans l'ombre,
Guidé par toi, je quitte mon réduit,
Je cours aux lieux où m'attend ma bergère ;
En nous voyant, la contrainte s'enfuit,
Et nous volons tous les trois à Cythère,
Avec l'essaim des aimables plaisirs.

Charmante Aglaure ! amante trop craintive,
O cher objet de mes brûlans desirs,
Prête à mes vers une oreille attentive ;
Je vais chanter les secrets d'un couvent.
Mais vous dévots, mais vous censeurs austères,
Que l'esprit saint égare si souvent,
Vous qui n'aimez que vos sottes chimères,
Gardez-vous bien de me lire un instant.

Non loin du Pô, sur un coteau stérile,
A quelques pas d'une superbe ville,
Soit par caprice, ou par religion,
Un vieux bigot bâtit un monastère :
Quatre vauriens, ne sachant trop que faire,
Vinrent loger dans la sainte maison ;
De capucins ayant déjà le nom,

Cette maison, par l'ignorant vulgaire,
Fut appelée une *Capucinière.*

Si je voulais suivre de point en point,
Un tas de lois qui gênent l'art d'écrire,
C'est bien ici le lieu de la décrire ;
Mais j'aime mieux ne la décrire point ;
On sait assez comment un monastère
Doit être fait pour loger des crasseux ;
Ainsi, je crois faire bien de me taire.

Là, quelques jours, ces fainéans heureux
Jouirent tous de la même puissance ;
Égaux entre eux, ils étaient fort contens,

Et vivaient même en bonne intelligence.
Ah ! cet accord ne dura pas long-temps :
Jamais la paix n'est entre gens d'église.

De ces vauriens, s'il faut que je le dise,
Le plus âgé ne comptait pas trente ans.
Trahi jadis par sa belle maîtresse,
Il prit le froc avec le nom d'Albin.
Le temps, bientôt, dissipa sa tristesse,
Et voulant être un parfait Capucin,
Il débuta comme un franc libertin,
En peu de temps surpassa ses confrères,
Et fut ainsi le premier de nos pères.

Les deux suivans, non moins mauvais sujets,
Pour éviter de faire la grimace
À ce poteau d'un si terrible accès,
Dirent au monde un adieu pour jamais,
En embrassant l'ordre de la besace ;
On les nommait père Jean, père Ignace.

Quant au dernier, je ne sais trop pourquoi
Il s'enrôla dans cette compagnie ;

Peut-être aussi fit-il quelque folie,
Toujours est-il qu'il s'appelait Éloi.

Sans autre droit que leur hypocrisie,
Le fondateur de la sainte maison
Les y maintint pour y dire l'office.
C'est donc ainsi que l'emporte le vice
Sur la vertu qui n'est plus qu'un vain nom !… »
O temps ! ô mœurs ! mais qu'y pouvons-nous faire ?…
Laissons le monde aller comme il voudra,
Heureux celui qui bien s'en tirera ;
Pour le moment ce n'est pas notre affaire.

En arrivant dans la Capucinière,
Le premier soin de nos quatre lurons
Fut d'enfermer, au fond du monastère,
Quelques beautés d'une humeur peu sévère.
On doit penser que ces jeunes tendrons,
Ainsi nichés avec de pareils merles,

N'étaient pas là pour enfiler des perles,
Mais bien… Suffit ; on m'entend ; poursuivons.

Dans un repas fait avec les donzelles,
Un jour Églé, (c'était une d'entr'elles),
L'esprit troublé par les vapeurs du vin,
Apostropha de ces mots père Albin :

« Dis donc, vieux chien, au nombre des pucelles,
As-tu juré de me laisser toujours ?
Tu le sais bien, je ne suis point farouche ;
Depuis trois nuits je partage ta couche,
Et cependant…

PÈRE ALBIN.

Brisons-là ce discours,
Point de mensonge, encor moins de colère.

ÉGLÉ.

Je ne mens point.

PÈRE ALBIN.

Bon, c'est assez, ma chère,
N'en parlons plus.

ÉGLÉ.

Mais…

PÈRE ALBIN.

Reçois ce baiser.

ÉGLÉ.

Oui, voilà bien tout ce que tu sais faire,
Prendre mes bras, me parler, m'embrasser,
Et rien de plus.

PÈRE ALBIN.

Tais-toi…

ÉGLÉ.

Je veux tout dire :
Certes ! crois-tu toujours en imposer ?… »

Ici chacun, par des éclats de rire,
Interrompit l'orateur emporté,
Et père Albin parut déconcerté.

    A la rougeur qui couvrait leur visage,
On se douta qu'Églé n'avait pas tort,
Et qu'en effet le père était trop sage.
Il veut parler, on rit encor plus fort.

    Tant de gaîté ne plaisait pas au père ;
Il trépignait de honte et de colère,
Jurant tout bas qu'il s'en vengerait bien :
« Messieurs, dit-il, au comble de sa rage,

Messieurs, messieurs, je suis votre doyen ;
Des ans sur vous n'ai-je pas l'avantage ?
Je tiens ici lieu de père garcien.
Obéissez : cette gaîté me lasse,
Et je prétends que l'on m'en débarasse.

PÈRE ÉLOI.

    « En vérité, l'ordre est assez nouveau ;
Comme il y va notre révérend père !
C'est fort bien fait de se mettre en colère,
De commander, mais d'obéir, tout-beau !

PÈRE ALBIN.

« Eh ! diable, aussi, faut-il croire une folle
Dont ce champagne a troublé le cerveau !

ÉGLÉ.

« Je suis donc ivre à t'entendre, bourreau !
Tu voudrais bien qu'on te crut sur parole.
Ah ! je suis ivre ; eh bien ! oui, je le sui ;
Mais non de toi, Capucin à la glace.
Va, je l'ai dit, tu peux dès aujourd'hui,

Faire venir celle qui me remplace.
Jamais Églé ne te pardonnera
L'affront sanglant que tu fais à ses charmes… »
Elle se tut ; et pour cacher ses larmes,
La pauvre enfant de ses mains se voila.

A peine eut-elle achevé ce reproche,
Que l'œil en feu, le visage irrité,
Albin courut sur la jeune beauté,
Pour lui donner quelque bonne taloche ;
Mais c'est en vain : les compagnes d'Églé,
Prirent parti contre l'écervelé,
Et leurs amis qui voyaient que l'affaire,
S'échauffant trop, aurait mauvaise fin,
Se mirent tous entre elle et père Albin.

Ici, sans doute, eût fini cette guerre,
Quand, par malheur, la petite Suson,
(Celle qu'Éloi chérissait davantage)
En avançant le bout de son visage,
Reçut, d'Albin, la confirmation,
Mais de manière à s'en guérir l'envie.

Ah ! qui pourrait redire sans effroi,
Dans quel transport entra le père Éloi,
Voyant ainsi souffleter son amie ?
Les léopards, les tigres, les lions
Sont des agneaux, si nous les comparons
A ces vauriens qui déjà sont aux prises.
Les coups de poing volent de toutes parts :
On jure, on peste, on se dit des sotises ;
Et la fureur anime leurs regards.

Tandis qu'ainsi la bataille s'engage,
Le grand François, leur bienheureux Patron,
Se promenant, assis sur un nuage,
Juste au-dessus de la sainte maison,
Entend les cris des femmes renversées,
Les juremens des quatre furieux,
Roulant parmi les bouteilles cassées ;
Et croit devoir descendre sur les lieux.

Tels qu'à l'aspect d'un pédant de collége,

Qui, tout-à-coup, vient reprendre son siège,
Trente marmots, criant tous à la fois,

Rentrent soudain dans un profond silence ;
Tels, en voyant paraître Saint-François,
Nos combattans levèrent la séance,
Pour se jeter, d'un air respectueux,
Aux saints genoux du Patron bienheureux.

Puisqu'ils y sont, qu'ils fassent pénitence.
Pour un instant, je suspends mes travaux :
Je ne veux pas trop fatiguer ma veine ;
Elle est peu forte, il lui faut du repos,
Et c'est ici que je reprends haleine.

Les Plaisirs de l'ancien régime, et de tous les âges,
Illustration.

Tandis qu'à terre, en le suivant des yeux,
Tous nos vauriens lui criaient : Bon voyage.

CHANT SECOND.

Que les couvens, dans ce siècle pervers,
Sont différens de ce qu'ils devraient être !
Ah ! si d'eux tous j'étais l'unique maître,
Sans balancer, au fin fond des enfers,
Dès aujourd'hui, je vous enverrais paître
Les animaux qui s'enferment dedans,
Pour s'engraisser et vivre à nos dépens.
Du vice impur, un cloître est le repaire.
Dans les couvens, que ne se fait-il pas ?
J'ai vu, j'ai vu des moines scélérats,
Au nom d'un Dieu qui ne les gène guère,
S'abandonner aux plus affreux excès…
Et l'on dira qu'il faut qu'on les révère !
C'est fort bien dit : mais moi qui les connais,
Je vous soutiens qu'il vaudrait mieux les craindre.

Confus, tremblans, aux pieds de Saint-François,
Nos champions étaient vraiment à peindre,

Quand père Albin, en assez fin matois,
Pour esquiver sa première boutade,
Prend la parole, et préludant trois fois,

Adresse au Saint cette capucinade,
Qui tint long-temps tous nos sots ébahis :

     « Très-saint Patron, ne soyez pas surpris,
Si, dans ces lieux, un apparent désordre
Sur vos enfans semble donner à mordre ;
Nous connaissons vos rigoureuses lois ;
Au fond du cœur chacun de nous les porte :
Mais ne peut-on s'en écarter par fois ?
La chair est faible, à moins qu'elle soit morte ;
Et vous voyez, très-révérend Patron,
Qu'aucun de nous n'est près de rendre l'ame.
Sans compromettre et l'Ordre et votre Nom,
Sans trop manquer à la Religion,
Ne pouvons-nous caresser une femme,
Nous quereller, pourvu que le secret
Meure avec nous dans notre monastère ?
Le ciel doit-il nous en faire un forfait ?
Le mal n'est mal qu'à l'instant qu'on le sait,

Et c'est un bien s'il demeure un mystère.
J'entends par mal celui que nous faisons,
En nous livrant à ces jolis tendrons,
En nous battant, en faisant bonne chère ;
Car je sais trop que si, dans nos couvens,
On oubliait de dire son bréviaire,
De réciter en commun la prière,
De marmotter des mots vides de sens,
Aux pieds du Christ ou de Sainte-Marie,

Ce serait fait de la seconde vie.
Hélas ! je suis peut-être dans l'erreur.
Sur tout ceci, se tromper est facile ;
Mais vous pouvez devenir mon sauveur :
Très-saint Patron, faites que dans mon cœur,
La vérité se choisisse un asile. »
Il dit, et baise avec soumission,
Le saint orteil du révérend Patron.

    À ce discours qui le faisait morfondre,
Le grand François ne sait trop que répondre ;
Il recueillit cependant ses esprits,
Toussa, cracha, s'essuya la moustache,

Et répondit : « *In nomine Patris*,
Tant de raison me confond et me fâche ;
Mais, mon cher frère, êtes-vous le Gardien ?
Avec lui seul je veux un entretien ;
Puis, je verrai ce que je dois vous dire.

PÈRE ALBIN.

    « Excusez-nous, très-révérend Patron :
Jusqu'à ce jour, sans songer à l'élire,
L'égalité régna dans la maison,
Aucun de nous n'est au-dessus des autres,
Et nous vivons comme les bons Apôtres,
Au jour le jour, et sans plus de façon.

« Point de Gardien ! le cas est punissable :
J'en suis fâché ; vous manquez à la loi,
Et là-dessus je suis inéxorable.
Point de Gardien ! mais voyons donc pourquoi
Vous trouvez bon de changer ainsi l'ordre ?
C'est sur cela que l'on pourrait bien mordre.
Mangez, buvez, battez-vous, ce n'est rien ;

Ayez chacun deux, trois, quatre donzelles,
Au fond ce sont de pures bagatelles,
Et dans le ciel nous nous en moquons bien.
Mais un couvent sans un père Gardien !
Oh, c'est trop fort ! Vous irez aux galères,
Ou tout au moins dans quelques séminaires.
Point de Gardien ! je n'en puis revenir…
Allons, allons, il faudra vous punir,
Et je m'en charge ; entendez-vous, chers pères ?

Père Jean.

« Quoi ! se peut-il ! eh quoi ! très-saint patron,
Vous permettez de caresser des filles,
D'être emporté, gourmand et biberon ;
Vous tolérez cent autres peccadilles :
Mais pour savoir nous passer d'un Gardien,

Vous nous voulez punir du séminaire !
Souffrez au moins…

Saint-François.

           Non, je ne souffre rien.
Me croyez-vous encore de la terre ?
Du Paradis je suis un habitant ;

Et certes là nous pensons autrement
Que lorsqu'ici nous jouons notre rôle.
J'ai, comme vous, aimé le cotillon ;
Dans mon printemps j'étais un bon luron,
Je préférais faire la rocambole
A l'abstinence, à ce jeûne fatal,
Qui m'a sitôt conduit en l'autre monde.
Mais, dans les bras d'une petite blonde,
Ayant gagné je ne sais trop quel mal,
Je fis le vœu d'être un saint personnage ;
(Voyez à quoi tient notre sainteté !)
Et je le fus, soit dit sans vanité.
Mais à présent, ah ! combien j'en enrage !
Que je maudis mon imbécilité !
J'aurais pu vivre au moins quelques années,
Je n'ai joui que de quelques journées !
Je fus un sot ; il n'en faut plus parler.
Le Paradis devrait m'en consoler,
Me direz-vous. Vraiment, belle fadaise !
Que fait-on là ? L'on admire Jésus,

27

On bâille, on dort, on s'ennuie à son aise ;
Mais l'on se dit : Nous sommes les élus.

Et puis d'ailleurs, sans mainte simagrée,
On peut fort bien s'en ménager l'entrée.
En Paradis, j'ai trouvé des pendus,
Des huguenots, des juifs, des philosophes,
Que sais-je, moi ? J'en fus scandalisé.
— Quoi ! dis-je alors, de semblables étoffes
Sont en ces lieux ? Que j'étais insensé !
Qu'ont-ils donc fait pour échapper au diable ?
— En trépassant, ils se sont confessés,
Répond Jésus, du ton le plus affable.
— Et puis ? — Rien autre. — Eh quoi ! C'en est assez ?
— Oui, sûrement ; tout dépend de la grâce.

   Vous le voyez, la chose saute aux yeux,
En Paradis, vous pourrez avoir place,
Sans, comme moi, vous rendre malheureux
Par continence, ou par coups de cilice.
Dans ce bas monde, il faut que l'on jouisse,
Pour que dans l'autre on se trouve un peu mieux.
Mais, au mépris des lois, des ordonnances,
Vivre cloîtrés, sans un père gardien,
C'est renverser l'ordre et les convenances ;

C'est me manquer : car, vous le savez bien,
J'ai fait ces lois, je les aime et j'y tien.

PÈRE IGNACE.

« Permettez-nous, je le demande en grâce,
Permettez-nous, très-révérend Patron,
Si ce n'est pas vous montrer trop d'audace,
D'oser vous faire une observation.
Notre maison est à peine achevée ;
On y travaille encore en mille endroits,
Et le soleil, depuis notre arrivée,
Sur l'horison n'a paru que trois fois.
Vous conviendrez que pour choisir un maître,
Premièrement, il faut se bien connaître.
Or, en trois jours cela ne se peut pas ;
Or, ce serait une grande injustice
De nous punir pour un semblable cas ;
Or, Saint-François a trop d'horreur du vice
Pour la commettre ; or, il excusera
Ce qu'en effet…

SAINT-FRANÇOIS.

Or, or, *et cœtera.*
Voilà des or, qui ne me plaisent guère.

Vit-on jamais un pareil orateur ?
Vous vous croyez apparemment en chaire,
Pour ennuyer ainsi votre auditeur.
C'en est assez, votre défense est bonne,
Relevez-vous ; Saint-François vous pardonne ;

Mais dans trois jour, souvenez-vous-en bien,
Que l'un de vous soit le père gardien,
Ou je me fâche, et de la belle sorte. »
Il dit et va pour enfiler la porte.

Soudain Églé, qui, jusqu'à ce moment,
En paraissant rêver profondément,
Avait gardé le plus triste silence,
Vers notre Saint, légèrement s'élance.

« — Homme de Dieu, lui dit-elle en pleurant,
Ayez pitié d'une fille séduite :
J'étais heureuse au fond de mon couvent ;
Ce débauché m'en fit prendre la fuite,
Ajouta-t-elle, en montrant père Albin ;
Depuis ce temps, je n'ai que du chagrin.
Hélas ! grand Saint ! à quoi suis-je réduite !

Quoi ! c'est Églé que l'on outrage ainsi ?
A dix-sept ans elle verse des larmes ;
A dix-sept ans elle est à la merci
De qui, grand Dieu ! d'un pareil sans-souci,
Qui la méprise et dédaigne ses charmes !
Ah ! c'est affreux, je n'y survivrai pas !
Oui, le cruel impunément m'outrage.
En le voyant, je m'étais dit tout bas :
Voilà celui qui, mieux qu'un jeune page,
T'enlevera ce bijou si vanté,
Que rarement on conserve à ton âge.

Réjouis-toi ; ce jour tant souhaité
Va luire enfin ; adieu ton pucelage.
Adieu !… Non, non ; il n'a pas seulement,
Depuis trois jours qu'il se dit mon amant,
Que je l'invoque et le presse et l'excite,
Daigné lui faire une seule visite.
Il est de glace… — Et vous êtes de feu,
Répond le Saint, en se prenant à rire.
Vraiment, je plains un si cruel martyre ;
Mais Calmez-vous, il finira sous peu.
Si père Albin vous outragea, ma belle,

Peut-être a-t-il bien moins de torts que vous.
Je le saurai : jusqu'alors filez doux.
Il est affreux d'être long-temps pucelle,
Je le sens bien ; mais vous l'avez voulu.
L'amour est juste ; il punit les coupables.
Vos doux forfaits sont pourtant excusables :
Toujours l'ennui marche avec la Vertu ;
Et quoiqu'on aime assez cette déesse,
On hait par trop son triste cavalier,
Pour se complaire à la suivre sans cesse.
Rien n'est cruel comme de s'ennuyer.

   Je disais donc que je puis vous absoudre ;
Mais il faudra pour cela vous résoudre
A conserver, jusqu'à demain matin,
Ce doux bijou qui cause votre peine :
Il est utile à mon pieux dessein.

Vous, mes gaillards, ajouta notre Saint,
Si vous voulez qu'en ces lieux je revienne
Vous apporter ma bénédiction,
Et faire en tout prospérer la maison,
Veillez sur elle, et de son pucelage

Assurez-vous qu'on ne tâtera pas.
Adieu ; demain, j'en dirai davantage. »

  Il dit et fait deux ou trois entrechats ;
Attrape ainsi le bout de son nuage,
Et s'élançant dans ce bel équipage,
Touche bientôt à la voûte des cieux,
Tandis qu'à terre, en le suivant des yeux,
Tous nos vauriens lui criaient : Bon voyage.

Chant 3.   *Pl. IV.*

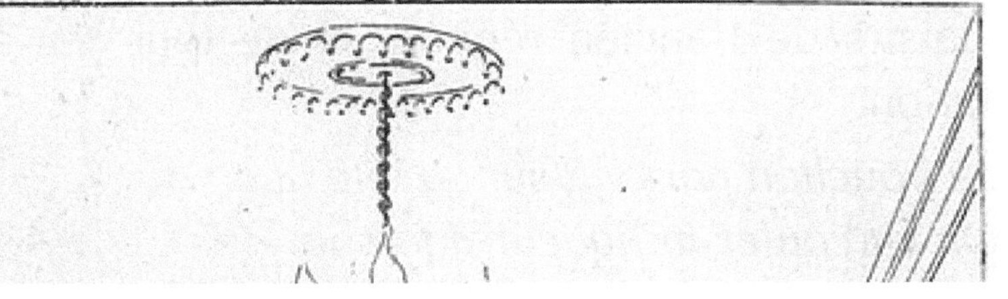

Les Plaisirs de l'ancien régime, et de tous les âges,
Illustration.

Le bouchon part, et, sur sa tête nue,
On vit couler la liqueur à foison.

CHANT TROISIÈME.

Corrigez-vous, Muse, corrigez-vous ;
Au nom de Dieu, prenez plus d'équilibre ;
Dans vos discours, vous êtes par trop libre.
On en murmure ; et les sots en courroux,
Jurent déjà qu'ils me feront occire.
A quoi sert-il de les désespérer ?
Ignorez-vous que pour avoir fait rire,
Plus d'une muse est réduite à pleurer ?
Eh ! que vous font ces animaux vulgaires ?
A la bonne heure, on peut s'en amuser ;
Mais gardez-vous de les scandaliser
En plaisantant du culte de nos pères.
Tout dans ce monde a son utilité.
Laissez en paix leur sainte trinité :
On sait fort bien qu'un si plaisant mystère
Est tout au moins une folle chimère.
Laissez en paix et leur Vierge-maman,
Et Saint-François et Saint-Pierre et Saint-Jean.

N'avons-nous pas d'autres sujets de rire ?
Et puis, voyons à quoi mène d'écrire

Ce que maint autre écrirait mieux que nous ?
Oui, je le sais, ce passe-temps est doux ;
Mais puisqu'enfin on y trouve à redire,
Corrigez-vous, Muse, corrigez-vous.
Quittez, quittez cette Capucinière
Qui déshonore à la fois vos pinceaux,
Et fait crier les prêtres et les sots.
Venez, qu'Amour nous conduise à Cythère.
C'est aujourd'hui la fête de sa mère ;
Tous les plaisirs vont voler en ces lieux,
Et vous pourrez y célébrer mes feux ;
J'y veux aussi conduire ma bergère. »

C'était ainsi que, tremblant pour mes jours,
Je suppliais ma muse trop hardie
De ménager un peu plus ses discours,
Et de me suivre en cette île chérie,
Où, se livrant sans contrainte aux amours,
Du peuple sot, on brave la furie.
Soins superflus… Je ne pus rien gagner.

Ah ! Puisqu'ainsi la cruelle s'obstine
A me vouloir conduire à ma ruine,
Bongré, malgré, je dois m'y résigner.
Hâtons-nous donc de reprendre une histoire
Que bien des gens ne voudront jamais croire,
Et c'est pourtant la pure vérité.

Quand notre Saint quitta le monastère,

Pour retourner où la Divinité
Fit de tout temps sa demeure ordinaire,
Déjà la nuit, d'un pas précipité,
Venait dans l'ombre envelopper la terre.
En ce moment, dans l'île de Lemnos,
Le noir Vulcain suspendait ses travaux ;
Mais sa moitié, qui chérit le mystère,
Se préparait à commencer les siens.

   Du grand François, les dernières paroles
Ne plurent guère à nos pieux vauriens.
« — En vérité, je les trouve assez folles,
Dit pere Jean, en s'approchant d'Églé ;
Notre Patron est, je crois, endiablé.

Un tel minois, avec son pucelage,
Est un ragoût dont je suis fort friand.
J'en veux tâter. Allons, ma belle enfant,
Sans plus tarder, mettons-nous à l'ouvrage.
Si notre Saint se fâche de cela,
Ma foi tant pis, il se défâchera.
Impunément vous ne serez pucelle. »
Il dit, et vole où son ardeur l'appelle.

   Mais père Albin, qui voyait son projet,
Frémit de honte ; il l'arrête, et lui crie :
« — Modérez-vous, mon frère, je vous prie ;
Ce doux bijou m'appartient, comme on sait.
— Eh pourquoi donc n'en faites-vous pas usage ?

Ce n'est pas là, (vous l'avez entendu),
Ce n'est pas là de ce fruit défendu
Qui perdit Ève à la fleur de son âge.
Servez-vous-en, je n'y toucherai pas.
Mais gardons-nous de laisser sans culture
De votre Églé les innocens appas ;
Car ce serait outrager la Nature,
Et mériter les vengeances du Ciel. »

Tout en parlant, père Jean, à l'autel,
Adroitement introduisait le prêtre…
Déjà du poste, il pense être le maître ;
Mais, ô miracle ! ô regret trop senti !
Le prêtre tombe… il semble anéanti…

Muse, dis-moi quelle fut la surprise
De père Jean, d'Églé, des spectateurs ?
Peins-moi leurs ris, leurs dépits et leurs pleurs :
De tels tableaux font honneur à l'Église.

Vous avez vu quelque fois un acteur,
Se reposant sur un mauvais souffleur,
Demeurer court au milieu d'une pièce,
Vous avez vu comment, à son malheur,
Tout un parterre entrait en allégresse,
Et par-là même augmentait son tourment,
Et l'embarras de sa jeune maîtresse,
A qui pour-lors il peignait sa tendresse,

En lui jurant de l'aimer constamment.
Tels à peu près, dans ce moment funeste,
La jeune Églé, père Jean et le reste
Renouvelaient ce spectacle plaisant.

Mais dans les airs, une cloche ébranlée
A, cependant, de son lugubre son,
Fait souvenir à la sainte assemblée
Qu'il était temps de dire le *Pardon*.
Tous, aussitôt, pleins de dévotion,
Font de la croix le signe salutaire,
Et, de concert, entonnent la prière
Faite en l'honneur de l'incarnation.

Cet *oremus* dit avec onction,
De père Jean dissipa la colère.
Sans lui, peut-être, en nouvel Illion,
Elle eût changé notre Capucinière.
Certes, alors j'étais dans de beaux draps,
Moi qui ne sais que chanter les combats
Du Dieu charmant qu'on adore à Cythère,
C'en était fait, pour sortir d'embarras,
Il eût fallu tout uniment me taire,
Ou devenir un des singes d'Homère,
Et ce choix même était embarassant ;
Mais c'est assez, revenons au couvent.

Las ! père Jean, honteux de sa disgrâce,
Ne savait trop s'il l'avoûrait ou non.

Un capucin ne manque pas d'audace ;
Mais sur l'article il est souvent Gascon,
Et convenir d'avoir trompé l'attente
D'une pucelle amoureuse et charmante,
C'est un aveu que le plus déhonté
Ne ferait pas sans rougir de lui-même.

    « — Ah ! je le vois, dit Albin enchanté
De l'embarras du nouveau Nicodème,
Tu te répens de ta témérité.
Allons, mon frère, Albin est un bon diable ;
Oublions tout, et reprends ta gaîté.
Quoiqu'on en dise, après avoir raté,
Un capucin peut être encore aimable.
N'en parlons plus, et viens te mettre à table. »

    C'était la règle, on sonnait l'*Angelus*,
Et l'on voyait voler au réfectoire,
Un marmiton qui se couvrait de gloire
En leur servant un repas de Crésus.
Quoique quêteurs, vous pouvez bien m'en croire,

Nos capucins étaient des mieux pourvus,
Il est encor tant de si bonnes ames,
Non pas chez nous, mais du moins chez nos femmes,
Que de long-temps ces méprisables gueux
Ne cesseront d'engloutir à toute heure,
Ce qu'on refuse à mille malheureux,
Qui, par la faim, chassés de leur demeure,

Vont implorant des secours en tous lieux.

    Le mot *raté*, bien qu'il fût à sa place,
A père Jean fit faire la grimace.
Il ne dit rien ; mais, dans le fond du cœur,
Il se promit qu'il en aurait vengeance.
Car tel est l'homme : il sourit à l'erreur,
Et bien souvent la vérité l'offense.

    Le souper prêt, vous jugez bien, je pense,
Qu'on s'empressa d'aller lui faire honneur.
De nos vauriens, le jeûne et l'abstinence
N'étaient connus que pour en rire entr'eux.

    Mangeant toujours, et buvant encor mieux,
Jusqu'au dessert on garda le silence,

Non que ce soit l'ordre de Saint-François ;
Mais vous savez qu'on ne peut à la fois,
En plein repas, manger, parler et boire :
C'est par abus qu'on le souffre au dessert.
Dès qu'il parut, ce fut un beau concert :
Chacun semblait se disputer la gloire
De ne rien dire, en discourant toujours ;
Tels que ces fats, vrais moulins à parole,
Petits faiseurs de fades calembours,
Qui, trop souvent, dans un cercle frivole,
Ont l'avantage, ou de nous endormir,
Ou d'ennuyer, si l'on y peut tenir.

Tandis que tous jasaient sans se comprendre,
Le père Ignace, un peu plus rafiné,
Gardait encore un silence obstiné ;
Mais, tout-à-coup, sa voix se fit entendre.

« Çà, mes amis, il faut parler raison,
Dit-il d'un air à leur en faire accroire,
Nous sommes tous jaloux de notre gloire,
Et de l'honneur de la sainte maison.

Or, écoutez ce que de nous exige
Un sentiment qui certe est des plus beaux :
La jeune Églé, sans doute, est un prodige ;
Ainsi, c'est clair, nous passerons pour sots,
Si, par malheur, on apprend que la belle
A, parmi nous, resté trois jours pucelle.
Passer pour sots ! mes Frères, songez-y.
Deux d'entre nous ne sont plus dignes d'elle ;
Mais je lui reste, Éloi lui reste aussi,
Et je puis bien me vanter, Dieu merci,
Que l'un des deux n'a bronché de sa vie.
Notre honneur donc exige qu'à l'instant
On dépucelle une si belle enfant.
Je l'avoûrai, j'en ai conçu l'envie ;
Mais ce soin-là regarde encore Éloi ;
Et je consens, pour éviter querelle,
Qu'Églé choisisse entre le père et moi.

ÉGLÉ.

Voilà parler ; combien j'aime ton zèle !
Ah ! père Ignace, ah ! je me donne à toi.

PÈRE ALBIN.

Que dites-vous ? quoi donc, Mademoiselle,
Vous vous donnez sans avoir mon aveu !
Non, s'il vous plaît, modérez ce beau feu ;
Moi, je prétends qu'on me reste fidèle.

PÈRE IGNACE.

Fi donc, mon cher, fi donc, tu fais l'enfant :
Songe à l'honneur de notre monastère.
Écoute, Albin, je suis accomodant ;
Cède-la moi ; je te céderai Claire.

PÈRE ALBIN.

De tout mon cœur. Le cas est différent,
Mon cher ami ; c'est une affaire faite.
Prends mon Églé : ta Claire m'appartient.

42

Père Éloi.

Non, s'il vous plaît ; ce marché ne vaut rien ;
Ne croyez pas que l'on vous le permette :
J'y mets obstacle, au nom de notre Saint.
Vous le savez, d'Églé le pucelage
Est nécessaire à son pieux dessein :
Ce sont ses mots. Il doit demain matin
Nous en apprendre, a-t-il dit, davantage.
Attendez donc.

Père Albin.

       Que j'attende ! Je crois
Que vous pensez que votre cervellette
Doit me dicter les lois de Saint-François.
Mais réprimez cette ardeur indiscrette :
Autant que vous je respecte ses lois ;
Et si j'y manque, en troquant ma maîtresse,
Un sot blanc-bec, soit dit sans vous troubler,
Ferait fort mal de venir s'en mêler.

Père Éloi.

Blanc-bec vous-même, impertinente espèce !
Nous allons voir si je suis un blanc-bec. »

Il dit, et paf : Maint et maint martin-sec
Sur père Albin tombent comme la grêle.
A cette attaque et plaisante et nouvelle,
Albin ne peut contenir sa fureur.
D'une bouteille il s'arme avec colère,
Recherche et joint l'insolent agresseur ;
Pour le frapper, il lève son tonnerre…
Mais, ô prodige ! admirez, comme moi,
Ce qui sauva de ses coups père Éloi.

Albin, trop prompt à saisir la bouteille,
N'avait pas vu qu'une liqueur vermeille
La remplissait jusques à son bouchon.
En s'en servant, comme d'une massue,
Le bouchon part, et, sur sa tête nue,
On vit couler la liqueur à foison.
Vous comprenez qu'un semblable baptême
L'arrêta court, et qu'il ne put lui-même
Ne pas en rire avec les spectateurs.

Mais cependant l'amoureux père Ignace
Pressait d'Églé les charmes enchanteurs.
Déjà le drôle espérait que la place
Se trouverait bientôt échec et mat.
Vaine espérance… Il est hors de combat.

« Oh ! pour le coup, je ne sais plus qu'en dire,
S'écrie Éloi, n'en pouvant plus de rire.

Quoi ! père Ignace !… Oh ! c'est par trop plaisant.
Allez, allez vous reposer, beau Sire ;
Vous en avez grand besoin sûrement.
Mais, pauvre Églé ! que je plains ton martyre !
Une autre fois choisis mieux ton amant.

— Plaignez-la moins, lui répond père Ignace ;
Et pour avoir le droit de plaisanter,
Entrez en lice ; on vous cède la place.
— Soit, répond-t-il, je veux bien l'accepter ;
Mais seulement pour vous couvrir de honte.
Çà dépêchons, ma belle, s'il vous plaît ;
Vous allez voir si j'ai bien fait mon compte. »
Il dit, et… Dieux ! son malheur est complet.

Ah ! comment rendre une scène si belle ;
Comment vous peindre et l'indignation,
Et la douleur, et la confusion
Du père Éloi, de l'aimable pucelle ?
Comment, comment répéter les bons mots,
Les quolibets et les plaisans propos
Qu'on dit alors dans la Capucinière ?
Mais nos cafards ne s'en tinrent pas là :
Chacun voulut recommencer l'affaire,
Et de nouveau chacun d'eux échoua.

« C'est singulier, dit encor père Ignace.
— Très-singulier, répéta père Albin,
Et je crains bien d'y perdre mon latin.

— En vérité, ce prodige me passe ;
Mais n'est-ce pas un tour de Saint-François,
Dit père Jean ? — Eh ! vraiment je le crois,
Répond Éloi : le drôle en est capable ;
C'est lui, sans doute, ou, ma foi, c'est le diable,

Enfin, voyant leurs efforts superflus,
Il fallut bien avaler la pilule.
Tous quatre donc, l'air piteux et confus,
A petits pas gagnèrent leur cellule,
Non sans pester de se voir *à quia*,
Non sans maudire et leur sort ridicule,
Et Saint-François, et tout ce qu'on voudra.

 *Chant 4* 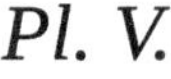 *Pl. V.*

Les Plaisirs de l'ancien régime, et de tous les âges,
Illustration.

Deux Séraphins le tenaient par l'oreille,
Précisément à deux pieds du plancher.

CHANT QUATRIÈME.

HEUREUX cent fois qui trouve un pucelage,
A dit Voltaire. Hé bien, il se trompait.
Mais cette erreur est celle du bel âge ;
Et dans un temps, mon cœur la partageait.
Ah ! chaque jour, la vérité cruelle
Vient nous ravir des mensonges charmans,
Et nous voyons sur les ailes du temps,
Tous nos plaisirs ainsi détruits par elle.

Mais de Phébus, les coursiers matineux
N'étaient encor lancés dans la carrière,
Que Saint-François, bien plus diligent qu'eux,
Avait déjà traversé tous les cieux,
Pour arriver à la Capucinière.
Il y trouva ses disciples ronflant.

« Comment, dit-il en frappant à la porte,
Personne ici ne veille en m'attendant ?
Voilà des gars d'une plaisante sorte ;
C'est, par ma foi, me traiter sans façons ;
Mais un moment, nous les éveillerons. »

Il dit, et fait quatre pas en arrière,
Prend son élan, et repoussant la terre,
Le Grand François est au haut du clocher.
D'une lucarne, il cherche à s'approcher,
La joint bientôt ; puis, la tête première,
Le Saint Patron s'y glisse de son mieux,
Non sans, pourtant, s'écorcher le derrière.

A peine est-il tout entier dans ces lieux,
Qu'un gros bourdon sonne à grand bruit matines :
Et c'était lui qui, d'un bras vigoureux,
Faisait mouvoir mesdames Jacquelines[2].
À ce concert des plus harmonieux,
Georges, sonneur de la Capucinière,
Se met en marche ; et bouillant de colère,
Fond sur le Saint, et, sans plus de façon,
Fait sur son dos danser martin-bâton,
Oh ! mais danser, de la belle manière.

« Au meurtre ! au meurtre ! au vol ! à l'assassin !
Finissez donc, laissez-moi, dit le Saint ;
Ah ! finissez, ou craignez la pareille. »
Mais le battant faisait la sourde oreille,
Et le battu poussait des cris en vain.

Le bruit, pourtant, de cette étrange scène,
Fort à propos, réveille père Éloi.
Une vieille arme aussitôt il dégaine :

Il part, il vole, il est dans le beffroi.

    La scène alors était bien différente :
Ce fier sonneur, d'une humeur si battante,
S'était calmé ; ne pouvant plus broncher.
Deux Séraphins le tenaient par l'oreille,
Précisément à deux pieds du plancher,
Et Saint-François, d'une ardeur sans pareille,
A tour de bras, sur son large fessier,
Lui remboursait, au vingtième denier,
Les mille coups que la sainte Excellence
Avait reçus de sa rare insolence.
En ce moment Éloi se présenta.
Ah ! s'il se peut, peignez-vous sa surprise.

En ris moqueurs d'abord elle éclata ;
Mais aussitôt, abjurant sa sottise :
« Quoi ! saint Patron, dit-il au Grand François,
Est-ce bien vous qu'en ces lieux je revois ?
Se pourrait-il que votre Seigneurie
Eût le projet d'attenter à la vie
D'un pauvre diable ?

Saint-François.

              Ah ! dites d'un bourru,
D'un insolent qu'à regret je ménage.
Je vous sonnais, et ce vrai malotru,
Sans dire mot, tout écumant de rage,

Vient, comme un trait, de grands coups de bâton
Me régaler.

PÈRE ÉLOI.

Eh bien ! très-saint Patron,
Pardonnez-lui ce moment de colère.

SAINT-FRANÇOIS.

Lui pardonner !

PÈRE ÉLOI.

N'est-il pas votre frère
Bien plus cent fois que ce chétif ânon,
A qui jadis vous donnâtes ce nom,
Lorsqu'en prêchant vous l'entendites braire.

SAINT-FRANÇOIS.

Bon, bon, alors j'étais ânon aussi,
Et puis j'avais mon personnage à faire.
Mais à présent, je suis saint, Dieu merci.
En saint, je veux punir son impudence.

51

Allons, coquin : que le diable à l'instant…

GEORGES.

N'achevez pas, ô des Saints le plus grand !
Si j'ai péché, c'était par ignorance.
En vérité, je vous pensais mortel ;
Ah ! sans cela, daignez, daignez m'en croire,
Georges, jamais, d'une action si noire
N'aurait voulu se rendre criminel.

SAINT-FRANÇOIS.

Mais tout au moins, tu pouvais bien, je pense,
Ne pas me battre avec tant de vigueur.

GEORGES.

Ignorez-vous que je suis un sonneur ?

SAINT-FRANÇOIS.

C'est autre chose. Eh bien ! fais pénitence,
Je te pardonne. » Il dit, et, sur-le-champ,
Les Séraphins lâchèrent ses oreilles.
Georges alors va, se les secouant,

Droit à l'église, où, près de quelques vieilles,
Il se prosterne, et marmotte tout bas
Des *oremus* que Dieu n'écouta pas,
Bien que pourtant il fit mainte grimace.

   Les Séraphins, ainsi que Saint-François
Et père Éloi, quittent aussi la place.
Les deux premiers gagnent le Ciel, je crois.
Pour les derniers, je vous le certifie,
C'est au couvent qu'ils reportent leurs pas.
Retournons-y, si nous ne voulons pas
Abandonner si bonne compagnie.

   Dans le clocher, tandis qu'on se battait,
Qu'on disputait, ou que l'on pardonnait,
Dans le couvent, à nos porte-besace,
La pauvre Églé de nouveau permettait
Le siège vain de l'imprenable place.
C'était pitié : Plein d'une noble audace,
Droit comme un I, l'assiégeant se montrait

Et, tout-à-coup, prêt à chanter victoire,
Triste et confus, sans vigueur, il tombait.

   « Bien ! dit le Saint, les prenant sur le fait,
Ah ! mes gaillards, vous manquez de mémoire.
C'est bon, c'est bon ; mais moi j'en ai pour tous ;
Et désormais, cherchez qui vous soutienne.
J'étais venu pour finir votre peine ;

Je ne veux plus qu'on me parle de vous ;
Adieu. Bientôt vous saurez s'il est doux
D'être l'objet de la plus grande haine
Qu'un Saint conçut dans son juste courroux. »
Il dit, et veut sortir du monastère ;
Mais père Albin le retient par un bras.

« Très-saint Patron, calmez votre colère ;
Ah ! s'il vous plaît, ne nous condamnez pas
Sans être sûr que nous soyons coupables.
Mais admettons que nous le soyons tous,
Vous le savez tout aussi bien que nous,
L'intention peut nous rendre excusables.
Or, apprenez qu'en cette occasion
Nous avons eu très-bonne intention.

Au fond d'un cloître, ainsi que dans le monde,
Règne un tyran que personne ne fronde
Impunément. De tout il est moteur.
Bon gré, malgré, chacun, à sa manière,
Aveuglément l'encense et le révère.
Le fastueux le met dans la grandeur ;
Le conquérant, à dépeupler la terre ;
Le philosophe, à rire à nos dépens ;
Le libertin, à tromper l'innocence ;
Et nous enfin, quoique le sage en pense,
A maintenir, en tous lieux, en tout temps,
L'opinion que l'insensé vulgaire
Veut bien avoir d'une Capucinière.

Ce tyran donc, que l'on appelle *Honneur,*
En nous soufflant son poison enchanteur,
Nous a forcés de manquer de mémoire.
Mais, ô grand Saint ! le pourrez-vous bien croire ?
La jeune Églé, malgré cette impudeur,
En ce moment est encore pucelle. »

    Ainsi parla le révérend Albin ;
Et Saint-François demeurait incertain.
Il se frotta quelque temps la cervelle,
D'un air rêveur, ou plutôt hébété ;
Puis, s'écria, s'adressant à la belle,
« A-t-il dit vrai ? — Très-vrai, répondit-elle.
Depuis l'instant que je vous ai conté
De mes malheurs l'histoire trop fidèle,
Hélas ! tous quatre ont vainement tenté
De mettre fin à ma longue misère. »
Églé se tut, et Saint-François reprit :
« Ma chère enfant, vous paraissez sincère ;
Mais je ne puis, dans une telle affaire,
M'en rapporter tout-à-fait au récit,
Permettez-moi d'aller jusqu'à la preuve.
— Je le veux bien ; mais à condition
Que j'obtiendrai, sitôt après l'épreuve,
De tant de maux la compensation.
— Sans contredit, je m'en rends caution. »

Mais notre Saint n'avait pas la science
Qui, chez Philippe, était un don du Ciel[3].

Il fut contraint, en semblable occurence,
D'agir en tout comme un simple mortel.
Ainsi d'Églé l'étonnant pucelage
Fut visité par le saint personnage :
Il le trouva parfaitement intact.
Alors, frottant de nouveau sa cervelle,
« C'est vrai, dit-il, le rapport est exact ;
La pauvre enfant est encore pucelle.
N'en doutons pas, ces profanes réclus,
Ainsi qu'Églé, n'en déplaise à la belle,
Dans leurs amours, ont outragé Vénus.
Pour vous punir, je devrais bien, mes frères,
Abandonner votre indigne maison ;
Mais Saint-François eut toujours le cœur bon ;
Je me souviens de mes fautes premières,
Et c'est pourquoi je vous excuse encor.
Écoutez-moi : Je vais vous parler d'or. »

Ici, le Saint fit une longue pause,
Et se moucha. Chacun en fit autant ;
Puis, il reprit : « Vous ignorez la cause
Qui fait qu'Églé conserve, en cet instant,
Son doux bijou. Par ma seule science,
J'ai pénétré ce mystère profond.
Plus d'une fois, vous avez fait faux bond
A la beauté : dans votre adolescence,

Moins délicats que pressés de jouir,
Chacun de vous a cherché le plaisir
Entre les bras d'une vieille coquette.
Plus d'une fois, au fond de sa couchette,
Notre pucelle a voulu que sa fleur
D'un vieux paillard ornât le front vainqueur.
Ce fut en vain : le triste octogénaire
N'en put jamais venir à son honneur.
Or donc, Églé, si le Dieu de Cythère
N'adoucit point ses arrêts rigoureux,
S'il reste encor long-temps sourd à nos vœux,
N'espérez pas que votre pucelage
Puisse, jamais, devenir le partage
De ces vauriens pleins de lubricité.
Oui, de l'Amour, telle est la volonté :
Lorsqu'une belle, à la fleur de son âge,
Voulut s'unir à de vieux libertins,
Elle ne peut cesser d'être pucelle

Par un amant aussi coupable qu'elle.
Mais j'ai sur vous le plus grand des desseins ;
En sa faveur, l'Amour vous fera grâce.
Ce monastère est sans père gardien ;
Votre bijou m'offre un plaisant moyen
D'en élire un digne de cette place,
Et je l'adopte. Ainsi, ma chère enfant,
C'est décidé ; vous et ces quatre pères,
Disposez-vous à me suivre à l'instant ;
Je me fais fort d'arranger vos affaires.

L'Amour n'est pas d'un si terrible accès :
J'en réponds donc, je ferai votre paix ;
Partons. » Il dit ; et le saint personnage
Fait aussitôt descendre son nuage.
Chacun s'y place, et tous, se trouvant prêts,
Un coup de vent emporte l'équipage.

Chant 5.   *Pl. VI.*

Les Plaisirs de l'ancien régime, et de tous les âges,
Illustration.

La voila donc le dos sur sa bedaine,
A nos paillards présentant ses appas.

CHANT CINQUIÈME.

Oui, c'en est fait, je veux me convertir :
L'impiété ne sied bien à personne ;
Un jour ou l'autre, il nous faudra mourir ;
Et savons-nous si le Dieu qui l'ordonne
Nous laissera le temps du repentir ?
Soyons dévots, c'est un parti plus sage ;
Le rôle en est peut-être fatigant.
Bon ! Chaque rôle a son désagrément ;
Mais n'a-t-il pas aussi son avantage ?
Nous ne devons songer qu'au dénoûment.
On n'est d'ailleurs que quelque temps en scène :
Par-ci, par-là l'on peut bien s'éclipser,
Et dans les bras d'une aimable mondaine,
Aller le soir, sans bruit, se délasser,
Sauf à s'en faire ensuite confesser.
Cette ressource est bien imaginée ;
Pour deux *Pater*, et peut-être un *Ave*,

Être lavé, mais proprement lavé
De cent forfaits commis en la journée,
Vous conviendrez que rien n'est plus charmant.
Ah ! servons-nous d'un si beau sacrement,
Et sur-le-champ ; nous ne saurions mieux faire.
Dès ce jour donc… Non, ce sera demain.
Un jour de plus ne fait pas une affaire :
Or celui-ci, j'irai le même train,
Je le consacre à la Capucinière ;
Mais pour demain, point de rémission,

Je tâterai de la confession.

    Vous le savez : non loin de la Morée,
Dans cette mer si célèbre autrefois,
Est de l'Amour la demeure sacrée.
Là, de ce Dieu, tout reconnaît les lois :
On n'y voit point de maîtresses cruelles,
D'époux jaloux, ni d'amans infidelles.
Aimer, le dire, et toujours le prouver,
Est, dans cette île, alors qu'on a su plaire,
Tout ce qu'on veut et tout ce qu'on sait faire.

Voilà des lois qu'il est doux d'observer !
Heureux ! heureux l'habitant de Cythère !
Dès qu'il s'enflamme, il n'a pas, comme nous,
A surmonter et grilles et verrous.
Les préjugés, ces tyrans du vulgaire,
Ne lui font pas à tout moment la guerre.
Il aime, on l'aime, il soupire, on se rend ;
Et ses désirs sans cesse renaissant,
S'augmentent même après la jouissance.
Hélas ! pourquoi dans nos tristes climats
L'Amour ainsi ne commande-t-il pas ?
Que n'étend-t-il une telle puissance
Du nord au sud, de l'aurore au couchant !
C'en serait fait : dès cet heureux instant,
Tout l'Univers quitterait tout pour elle ;
Et Mahomet et Jésus et Brama,
Et des sots dieux la longue kyrielle,

Pourraient fort bien dire : *Meâ culpâ.*

    De Saint-François le léger équipage,
En un clin-d'œil, conduisit dans ces lieux,

Lui, la pucelle et ses quatre amoureux.
En les voyant sortir d'un gros nuage,
L'Amour les prit tout au moins pour des dieux ;
Mais son erreur fut de courte durée.
Chacun le sait, et lui-même encor mieux,
Les habitans du céleste Empirée,
D'un capucin n'ont pas l'habit crasseux,
Ni l'air commun, ni la sotte tournure.
Toujours puant, et mal propre et brutal,
C'est beaucoup trop, lorsqu'un tel animal
A des humains conservé la figure.

    L'Amour leur dit : « Soyez les bien venus ;
Vous paraissez des soldats de Jésus,
Et je les aime ; or, puis-je en quelque chose
Vous être bon ? répondez-moi. — Je n'ose,
Dit Saint-François.

L'Amour.

           Pourquoi donc ? Un enfant
Vous effrairait ! Oh ! je ne suis terrible
Que lorsqu'un cœur veut rester insensible ;

Et vos habits me sont un sûr garant
Que je n'ai pas de plus zélés apôtres.
Parlez, parlez.

Saint-François.

De tout temps, en effet,
Les Capucins en ont bien valu d'autres :
Le monde entier est d'accord sur ce fait.
Aimable Enfant, dont j'ai dans ma jeunesse,
Pour mes péchés, trop peu suivi les lois,
A tes genoux, tu vois le Grand François…

L'Amour.

Comment, un Saint !

Saint-François.

Oui, j'ai cette faiblesse,
Et Jésus-Christ l'aurait tout comme moi.
Nous autres Saints, nous faisons, sans effroi,
Une folie, et même une sottise,
Quand c'est sur-tout pour le bien de l'Église :
Car c'est ainsi qu'on établit la foi.
Ah ! qu'en mon temps, j'en ai fait dans Assise,
Où je suis né. L'on disait : Il est fou !

63

Et je l'étais. Courant le guilledou,
J'ai… Mais ceci n'est pas trop à ma gloire.
N'en parlons pas. Aussi bien je ne veux
Te raconter mon incroyable histoire,
Mais t'implorer pour ces religieux,
Pour cette enfant en dépit d'eux pucelle.
Elle est coupable ; ils le sont autant qu'elle…

L'AMOUR.

Suffit, j'entends. Ma foi, tant pis pour eux.
Tes protégés, en manquant à ma mère,
M'ont outragé. Leurs méprisables feux
Méritent bien ce châtiment sévère.

SAINT-FRANÇOIS.

J'en suis d'accord ; mais je puis me flatter
Qu'en ma faveur tu leur en feras grace.
J'ai quelque droit pour la solliciter.
Au fondateur de la sainte besace,
Tu dois beaucoup : mes couvens sont tous pleins
De tes sujets, tous fieffés libertins.
Amour, c'est là qu'on te rend bien hommage !
Qu'au fond d'un cloître, on te brûle d'encens !}}

Qui sait le mieux satisfaire ses sens,
Passe chez nous pour être le plus sage.

64

L'AMOUR.

Jamais l'Amour ne sait rien refuser :
Je cède donc.

SAINT-FRANÇOIS.

Bravo ! bravo ! mes Frères :
De ce pardon il vous faut bien user,
Et le plutôt. Je n'en fais pas mystères :
Sur certains points, vous pouvez déroger
A mes statuts, et ne pas m'outrager :
Tout n'y doit pas être pris à la lettre ;
Mais, je l'ai dit, je ne saurais permettre
Qu'un seul couvent soit sans père gardien.
Le vôtre encore est à nommer ; hé bien,
Ceux d'entre vous qui désirent de l'être,
Vont essayer d'enlever, en courant,
Le doux bijou de cette aimable enfant.
Qu'en penses-tu, charmant Dieu de Cythère ?

L'AMOUR.

Que cette idée est bien digne d'un Saint !

SAINT-FRANÇOIS.

Mais, tout au moins, tu l'approuves, j'espère ?

L'Amour.

Certainement. Un si noble dessein
Me plaît beaucoup, et bien plus je l'admire.

Saint-François.

Admire donc ; mais garde-toi de rire.

« En vains discours ne perdons pas le temps ;
Allons, allons, Messieurs les concurrens,
Nuds comme un ver, qu'à l'instant on se mette ;
Et vous, Églé, point de sottes façons,
Dépouillez-vous de ce tas de chiffons,
Qui nous dérobe une jambe parfaite,
Un sein d'ivoire et ce charmant séjour
Fait tout exprès pour les jeux de l'amour. »

Enfin ici le Saint reprit haleine ;
Et nos vauriens, déjà prêts aux combats,
Se disputaient l'honneur du premier pas,

Tous à la fois voulaient entrer en scène,
Mais Saint-François réprima tant d'ardeur.

66

« Chacun son tour, dit-il avec douceur :
D'abord Albin ; puis Jean, ensuite Ignace,
Et puis Éloi. Chez nous, en fait d'honneur,
Les plus âgés ont la première place. »
Il dit : Bientôt, à l'aide de ses doigts,
Sort de sa bouche un bruit insoutenable.
On aurait cru qu'un chasseur aux abois
Sifflait après sa meute infatigable :
Et sur-le-champ, deux jolis Séraphins
Sont à ses pieds, baisant ses saintes mains.

Le Grand François, d'un air grave et capable,
Donne à chacun son rôle et son emploi.
« Amour, dit-il, tu seras Juge, toi.
Moi, je tiendrai la charmante pucelle ;
Les Séraphins debout, ainsi que moi,
S'empareront des jambes de la belle.
Vous, mes lurons, voilà votre chemin ;
Suivez-le bien : le reste est notre affaire.

Pour vous, Églé, votre rôle est divin !
Ne faites rien, mais laissez-vous tout faire. »
Il dit : Églé se jette dans ses bras.

La voilà donc le dos sur sa bedaine,
A nos paillards présentant ses appas.
Les Séraphins exécutent, sans peine,
L'ordre précis du révérend Patron ;
Et père Albin s'élance dans l'arène…

Hélas ! ce fut à sa confusion.
Son successeur aussitôt le remplace :
Comme un éclair il part… Même disgrâce….
L'autre en sourit, et regarde l'Amour.
Plein d'assurance, il s'élance à son tour…
Nouveau malheur… Il faut pourtant le dire :
Moins bien armé, le formidable sire
Eût mérité nos applaudissemens.
(Le don heureux ne l'est pas en tout temps,
Comme l'on voit). Vous présumez peut-être
Que pere Éloi va nous les arracher :
Attendez donc, vous allez le connaitre.

Éloi s'élance, Éloi… veut se cacher.
Son infortune anime ses confrères ;
Et tous les quatre ils redoublent d'ardeur.
L'un après l'autre, on vit ces pauvres pères
Sur la pucelle épuiser leur valeur.
C'en était fait : Elle en pleurait de rage,
Quand de nouveau, les cheveux hérissés,
Les yeux en feu, la luxure au visage,
L'air menaçant et les bras élancés,
Éloi revient où la gloire l'appelle.
Heureux mortel ! te voilà dans le port…
A ce succès, il sent croître son zèle.
Églé se trouble… Il s'agite sur elle,
La presse… Hélas ! un obstacle plus fort
Semble vouloir rendre vain son transport.
Plein de fureur, il serre alors la belle

En cent façons ; la pousse, la harcelle,
La serre encor, fait un nouvel effort…
Effort vainqueur ! Églé n'est plus pucelle !…
Au même instant, l'air retentit des cris
De vive Éloi ! vive le jeune père !

Et Cupidon, avec un doux souris,
Dit : « Grand François, il mérite le prix ;
Qu'il soit gardien de la Capucinière.
Il le sera, lui répond notre Saint ;
Il en est digne, et c'est bien mon dessein.
Sur ce, je pars. Adieu : l'heure me presse ;
J'aurais voulu demeurer quelqu'instant ;
Je ne le puis, il est tard, cher enfant,
Et pas un d'eux encor n'a dit sa messe.
Tu le vois donc, il est très-important
De regagner au plutôt le couvent. »
Il dit : Soudain, l'équipage ordinaire
Les reçoit tous. Un nouveau coup de vent
Vous les reporte à la Capucinière.

Pour cette fois, les suive qui voudra.
J'ai vu d'Églé prendre le pucelage ;
Il me suffit. *Amen, Alleluia* :
J'ai terminé mon saint et fol ouvrage.

O mon Aglaure ! ô toi qui jusqu'ici
Fus attentive aux accords de ma lyre,

Toi que je vis quelquefois y sourire,
Et plus souvent prête à me dire : Fi !
Ces rimes-là sont toutes à refaire.
Tu le veux donc ; il faut te satisfaire.
Dès que j'aurai corrigé mes enfans,
Un imprimeur en fera son affaire ;
Et si, contr'eux, les cagots, les pédans
Font éclater une sainte colère,
Je m'en rirai. Trop heureux si mes Chants,
A des lecteurs d'une humeur moins sévère,
Ont, comme toi, l'aimable don de plaire.

ÉPILOGUE.

Je l'ai promis, je vais me confesser,
Et c'est à vous, successeur de Saint Pierre,

Qu'il appartient de me débarrasser
Du lourd fardeau que je veux déposer.

« — Quoique bien jeune, hélas ! mon très-saint Père,
J'ai mérité le courroux du Seigneur.
Vous connaissez cette Capucinière !…
— Eh bien, mon fils ! — Eh bien ! j'en suis l'auteur.
— Vous avez fait cette œuvre abominable ?
— Oui, très-saint Père, elle me doit le jour :
Je me croyais inspiré par l'Amour,
Et, je le vois, je l'étais par le diable.

— Impie affreux ! vous irez en enfer.
— Je le crains bien, j'ai mérité la corde ;
Mais, cher Papa, je tiens d'un Magister,
Qu'à tout péché Dieu fait miséricorde ;
Et pourquoi donc ne pourrais-je espérer
De sa bonté cette preuve éclatante ?
— Vous le pouvez : mais, l'ame repentante,
Monsieur l'Auteur, il vous faut abjurer
Et prose et vers. — Mon Père !… — Il faut encore
Vous dépouiller de cet habit mondain,
Abandonner à jamais votre Aglaure,
Et, dès ce jour, vous faire capucin.
— Moi, capucin ! moi, quitter mon amie !
Moi, ne rimer, n'écrire de ma vie !…
Non, cher Pater, non je ne le puis pas.
Tant pis pour vous : la chose vous regarde ;
Votre intérêt vous dit d'y prendre garde.

Voyez l'enfer entr'ouvert sous vos pas…
Et ce fauteuil qu'à sa droite vous garde
Le bon Jésus. Osez-vous balancer ?
— Allons, mon père, il nous faut composer.
J'y consens donc ; je quitte le Permesse.

Je ferai plus : je lirai le Romain[4] ;
Mais laissez-moi mon aimable maîtresse,
Et renoncez à me voir capucin.
— Non ; tout ou rien. — Que vous êtes terrible !
Ah ! s'il vous plaît, daignez être plus doux.
Eh quoi ! grand Dieu ! ne vous est-il possible
D'avoir pitié d'un auteur à genoux ?
Adoucissez un peu la pénitence.
— Je ne le puis. — Ainsi donc, cher Pater,
Vous me voulez livrer à Lucifer ?
Songez-y bien : sur votre conscience
Je mets le crime. — Il n'en existe pas,
Du moins pour moi ; mais c'est trop de débats.
Allons, voyons, consentez-vous à faire
Ce que j'ai dit ; serez-vous capucin ?
— Mon père… — Ensuite ? — Hélas ! — Et puis ? Mon père,
Trouvez-le bon, je reviendrai demain. »

Le lendemain, cent fois plus incertain,
Au jour suivant je remis tout encore ;

Mais ce jour-là, je revis mon Aglaure…
Ivre d'amour, et mourant sur son sein,

Je m'écriai : C'en est fait, très-saint Père !
Oui, je veux bien me faire capucin,
Mais que ses bras soient ma Capucinière.

FIN

1. ↑ M. Geoffroy a dit dans son Feuilleton du 19 août 1807 : *Le progrès des lumieres nous a fait voir que toutes les religions sont aussi bonnes les unes que les autres ; que toutes les manières d'adorer Dieu, lui plaisent également, etc.*
2. ↑ Les cloches.
3. ↑ Saint Philippe savait reconnaître, en flairant une fille, si elle était pucelle, ou non. Voyez sa Vie.
4. ↑ Le *Bréviaire Romain*.